OUTSIDE-IN.

THE SECRET OF THE 21ST CENTURY LEADING COMPANIES.

By STEVE TOWERS

Foreword by

JOHN CORR

Business Process Group

(www.bpgroup.org)

Outside-In. The Secret of the 21st Leading Companies,
3rd Edition.

ISBN 978-0-9565135-0-2

Includes bibliographic references.

For bulk orders and educational requirements please contact
outsidein@bpgroup.org

For additional resources visit www.outsideinthesecret.com

Foreword

I've known Steve Towers for over 20 years, ever since we were both ambitious young senior executives at one of the UK's leading banks. He's been one of the most fun, warm, generous and inspiring people I've met in my adult life. A great family man and friend and the most knowledgeable person I can think of globally in terms of process management.

As the current President of the not-for profit BPGroup.org, arguably the leading specialist interest group on business performance with over 40,000 members globally - see us online at http://www.bpgroup.org it's been my pleasure to be invited to write this foreword.

By way of personal introduction, I'm currently a Director in the London offices of AlixPartners a global leader in helping organisations deliver turnarounds and transformations in their performance with clients such as General Motors, Dubai World and LyondellBasell. I've been privileged to work with some of the world's most remarkable business people who I've had the honour to help deliver some remarkable turnarounds and transformations of leading global businesses. These have included:

Philip Rowley (CEO of AOL Europe) in transforming losses of over $600 million per annum to profitability.

Andy Homer (CEO - AXA Insurance UK) turnaround losses of £100 million ($150 million USD) per annum to profitability. Subsequently Andy went on, as Group Chief Executive, to grow Towergate Insurance to become Europe's most valuable privately held Financial Services business worth over £3 billion in 5 years.

Joe Ripp (President - Dendrite International) to transform the value of a sophisticated outsourcing business and double its value (from $8 to $16 per share) within a year. Joe was previously CFO of Time Warner. To review these stories and more visit www.johncorr.com

So you may be interested in wondering why you should invest your precious time in reading this book, with all the pressures of the current business climate why will this investment be worthwhile?

I'd like you for a moment to think of 'high jumping'. This is a sport that has been pursued actively from the ancient Greeks in the original Olympics to modern times. And for nearly 3,000 years people jumped using similar techniques until an innovator, Dick Fosbery thought of a new approach that was incredibly simple and yet at the same time delivered 'breakthrough performance' levels enabling him to win the gold medal in the 1968 Olympic high jump competition. In retrospect, it was incredibly obvious that the most effective approach was to run up to the high jump bar and leap over it backwards overturning thousands of years of 'best practice'.

So I would like you to give yourself permission to consider that you too can achieve 'breakthrough performance' in your own business endeavours. In this book 'Outside In', Steve Towers will introduce you to some remarkable concepts, that at first seem simple and obvious, and yet when applied will allow you to win the gold medal in your own field of business.

John Corr (President of BPGroup.org)

London, April 2010

Acknowledgements

I wish to acknowledge the unstinting support of the BP Group and broader community in debating the issues and working diligently across the globe to move our organisations closer to the customer. In no small way I sincerely thank a very special group of people, the BP Group Advisors:

John Corr, Charles Bennett, Dick Lee, Sunil Dutt Jha, Dr. Fahad Altwaijry and David Mottershead.

Also a selection of the BP Group Certified Process Processional Masters (CPP Master) across 118 countries:

Marjolein Towler, Stephen Nicholson, Craig Reid, Martina Beck-Friis, Maria Möllersten, Janne Ohtonen, Nic Harvard, Erika Westbay, Paul Bailey, Rosalind Slaughter, Jayanthi Venkatachalam, Stephen Ferguson, Sandra Vincent-Guy, David Johnson, Neville Inglis, Adam Keens, Gerard Gillespie, Benoit Dubouloz, Caroline Holyhead, Sofie Smolders, Steve Graham, Simon Love, Helen Littlechild and Pete Marshall.

I am proud to call these 'Masters' my friends who all share a desire to make the planet a better place - transforming the world one person, one process, one organisation at a time. And last but not least to you the reader, thank you.

Introduction: Why I wrote this book

The world is experiencing a transformation like never before. Everything we thought we ever knew is being challenged and in some instances complete concepts, philosophy and the ways of living our lives turned upside down. This transformation is being played out in all our lives and especially so in the business world. Seismic shifts in the world order with previously dominant economies struggling to meet the demands of the 21st century. Meanwhile emergent economies are setting new benchmarks for performance and delivery and day by day change your and my expectations as customers.

As someone working actively with many of the world's leading companies I have a privileged first-hand experience of these shifts in approach and business strategy. I have participated and watched new approaches emerge and have seen these play out on the international stage.

It isn't only that the rules of the game have changed, this is a completely new game, with new players, new strategies and a new scoreboard. I call this collective shift 'Outside-In'. The Outside-In philosophy, basically recognizes that everything is a process and the only ultimate purpose of any process is to satisfy a customer need.

Some companies choose to use names such as customer centricity, advanced BPM, or transformation. However at their core, and for our purposes such approaches fit the Outside-In definition.

This book is therefore all about this Copernican shift, a refocusing of our organisations with the customer central to everything we do. It reviews the winning approaches, the immediate and actionable steps available to others who then understand the shift, and most importantly offers a practical hands-on route for those people and organisations wishing to join the successful companies of the 21st century.

It is a book to be read as you need it. Dip into the specific themes, explore the techniques and review at leisure. Share it with colleagues and join this exciting and exhilarating journey to Outside-In. You will never think of business in the same way again.

Enjoy your journey to Outside-In and seize the day

Steve Towers
London, April 2010

Table of Contents

***

ONE DAY during his
tenure as a professor,
Albert Einstein was visited by a
student.
"The questions on this year's
exam are the same as last
year's!"

Einstein answered,
"yes, but this year
all the answers are very
different."

***

New Answers to Old Questions

One of the key challenges facing businesses today is how to keep pace with, and preferably anticipate, the needs and expectations of customers. These expectations have changed as we have become better educated and informed about the buying decisions we make. We want the organisations that we do business with to show that they understand what we need and are able to deliver it. This demands flexibility and agility from the businesses that want to gain and keep satisfied customers. At the same time competition is growing: this era of globalization is seeing vibrant new economies emerging.

Asian countries are moving forward rapidly and dominating various markets. China is the fastest-growing major economy in the world, growing for the past 30 years with an average annual GDP growth rate of over 10%.

By 2020 the Indian economy will be the second largest in the world behind China. The world's largest Telco, based on subscribers, is based in China with more than 539 million customers[i]. Its nearest competitor, UK based Vodafone, struggling with administration issues is 110 million behind. And China Mobile has the Apple iPhone monopoly in China. So what? There is a new normal out there and the traditional ingredients for success do not apply anymore. You either get with the new game and begin answering some of the questions in a different way or you'll be left on the industrial scrap-heap.

Is there one single action plan for responding to this challenge? Good news - different industries are adopting similar themes that we can discern and in-turn make our own. These themes revolve around how we organise the work we do to achieve success. The leading companies understand the need to achieve Successful Customer Outcomes and accordingly question structures and ways of working that have remained largely unchanged since the industrial revolution. Let's review some of the critical areas.

What constraints are there on how the organisation is structured?

"We trained hard … but it seemed that every time we were beginning to form up into teams we would be reorganised. I was to learn later in life that we tend to meet any new situation by reorganising; and a wonderful method it can be for creating the illusion of progress while producing confusion, inefficiency, and demoralisation." Petronius, (27-66 AD) courtier to Emperor Nero.

This quote so eloquently describes most people's experience of company reorganisation. Unfortunately many organisations start with the internal structure when addressing a new challenge. The problem is that most organisations don't know enough about what they are trying to achieve before they embark on changing how they operate. Let's look at a couple of aspects of this:

Structures should exist to help make things happen, so it should be pretty clear from the outset what these important things are. Successful Customer Outcomes should be the basis for any organisation's activities, so structures should help do the right things rather than just making sure that things get done right. There are companies that set strict guidelines for how many hierarchical levels should exist and how wide spans of control should be, often linked to the limits of effective performance management. If a company performance management system has a big influence on team structures, then it's the performance management system that needs fixing.

It's no accident that the process tools commonly used to draw structure charts default to an arrangement of boxes joined by straight lines, with "bigger jobs" towards the top and team members arranged in a flat horizontal line left to right beneath. If these applications defaulted to a series of concentric

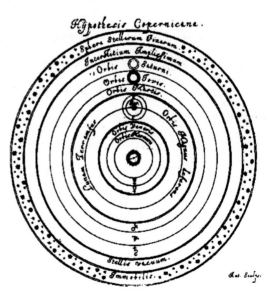

circles with the customer in the middle, might some organisations end up looking a little different? Where would the "big jobs" be? Would functions dominate the division of responsibilities or might customer-facing activities have more sway?

A Copernican shift

I like to think of the relationship between a business and its customer base as a solar system, where the customers act like the sun, influencing how the other parts work together. If our solar system functioned like most companies then planets would revolve around each other with the sun looking on in some bewilderment. So rather than trying to decide which of your organisation's planets (or functions) everything should revolve around, get it fixed in your mind that the energy and light-giving customer is at the centre of everything and allow the rest to follow from that.

Planets have it easy in one way - they have no option but to submit to the natural forces, such as gravity, that determine their orbits. Organisations, however, can choose to what extent they allow market forces to dictate how they operate. The best companies use these forces to propel themselves forward, and they do this by getting their people aligned with what they are trying to achieve, hence the next question:

How is success measured and rewarded?

Measuring the success of a business has to be more than just looking at the bottom line. Companies have to broaden their outlook and look beyond short term financial indicators. An important measure of a company's success must be its ability to improve performance continuously. Truly successful companies understand and actively manage what influences their people to do the right things every day. And the important phrase here is "do the right things".

If the performance targets are linked to non-customer focused corporate objectives then more and more dumb stuff gets done. Most objectives are inward-looking and often functionally specific, as are most of the staff reward mechanisms based on the traditional production mind-set of doing more things, working more quickly, fitting in well, playing the game. Put another way, their rewards are linked to an inside-out "doing something to something to get something". However where objectives are truly focused on Successful Customer Outcomes and people have the flexibility to do the right things, there is less need to impose so much structure on people. Organisation structures then become support mechanisms rather than control mechanisms.

The last question I want to pose is one that is crucial in differentiating between leaders and followers:

How is change pre-empted in the organisation?

Companies that have focused themselves on the customer, organised around that, and aligned their people appropriately have achieved most of what they need to be successful in the new world. However the leaders of these Outside-In companies are doing something else too – they aren't just reacting quickly to change, they are anticipating it and sometimes driving it themselves. To do this they have created working environments that generate forward leaps in innovation. When most organisations are consumed by reacting to crises, this is a distinct advantage.

Don't make the mistake of believing that this is the same as emulating the best practice of others, because this is no longer good enough. It has worked very well in the past, notably where the car industry was transformed by the widespread adoption of Japanese production techniques. The difference now is that customers are looking for added value, and simply following the rest isn't going to work. So rather than looking for best practice, companies need to be more innovative, and go beyond 'best' and look for 'next' practice.

So what should be done with the learning from these questions? Well here's a tip – don't start from what you do now and look for incremental improvement. Companies with a short-term and predominantly cost reduction outlook pursue a periodic crash diet approach to keeping themselves on target. What's needed now is a completely different approach – a healthy eating regime if you like, a permanent shift in habits and behaviours to get on the path to long term survival.

The gulf between the organisations that understand what Successful Customer Outcomes (SCO's) are and structure themselves around them, and those that carry on with same-old, same-old, is widening as we speak - in fact it's becoming a chasm. So if you're not working out how to get across that chasm now, you are going to be one of those organisations that get left behind, irrelevant. It just isn't good enough to get a bit better at what you are doing, the changes needed are fundamental. It's a new era and that means new answers.

Business Transformation – Are you on-board?

Synopsis

The world of business is undergoing dramatic change. Driven by a number of factors organisations are needing to realign themselves to adapt and evolve. This transformation is global and reaches into every business sector impacting how companies create, deliver and sustain their products and services.

Here we reiterate the reasons for the change, the size of the challenge and how some world leading trend setter companies are achieving dramatic success in this new order.

The current challenge

Everyone in business these days has learned their trade during the Information Age which arrived with the advent of mainframe computers in the 1960's. The transformation of the way we work, especially in services industries, was radical and gave birth to new ways of doing things that had remained largely unchanged since the invention of the steam engine. Alongside this information revolution a change came about in the way we organized business in order to exploit the advantages offered by automation. People talked of software and hardware; information systems; bits and bytes; system development; data processing. In fact this new way of doing work influenced every aspect of our lives and we adopted a predominantly left brain structured approach to organizing ourselves.

The very way we designed work became dominated by 'structured approaches' for systems development and management. Subsequently this information age mind-set grew its influence into work areas such as human resources, sales and marketing, operations and all the other 'functional areas' we are now very familiar with. The specialists in each of these respective functions, take Accounting for example, thought of their world through a lens provided by the information Age which ensured a structured methodical approach to change that would indeed harness the power of computers.

Everything became information centric. Think about this for a moment. What is the language you use in your particular discipline? For instance in Financial Management the talk may be of Activity Based Management systems, Budgetary control, Accounts reconciliation, purchasing, Cost Codes and such. All these things are underpinned by 'systems' and we draw structures that represent information processing. Companies like Oracle and SAP prosper in helping companies understand these functional controls and databases.

The things we do as work can also be represented as processes and these are conceived, developed and distributed through the information age lens. Swim lanes, functional hierarchies, business process management systems, process modelling languages and much more. Where has this all taken us?

To put it bluntly, it has taken us away from the customer who is, let's not forget, the very reason why our businesses exist in the first place. If you are involved in creating processes or systems think about the designs you produce. Where is the customer in those

'pictures' and designs? Customers are frequently an afterthought and at best at the 'beginning' or the 'end' of a process. We draw organisation models as pyramids and talk about the 'front line', interestingly customers are usually placed at the foot of the organisational pyramid. Our very ways of thinking isolate us from the customer and many can pretty much carry on with their functional objectives often without even thinking of the real customer as any more than something at the beginning or the end – nothing to do with them.

Where we have taken time to think about customers we have created 'Customer Relationship Management (CRM) systems' which are frequently islands of automation not fully integrated with back-offices – what is the 'back office' anyway? Groups of people remote from the customer, processing information and occasionally needing to deal with other parts of the organisation. Sometimes the apparent disconnects between different functional areas result in another initiative to 'outsource' work that is regarded as not being part of a core competence. Customers then end up talking to remote people sitting on the other side of the planet with mixed results.

Some people may argue that they do in fact deal with customers – those internal counterparts in other functions. We establish customer-supplier relationships, negotiate Service Level Agreements and busy ourselves with negotiations and agreed targets. Competition for scarce resources is the name of the game as we go into the annual round of bidding and corporate in fighting. Sounds familiar? Well you are not alone as this is the way of the Information Age mind-set.

Work has become so complex with the interconnection between people and systems that we seem constantly to be reinventing projects to 'sort out the mess' however our efforts are stilted by this very complexity with unfulfilled promises of new systems and improved ways of working. It just gets even more complicated.

There is a New Way - Outside-In

Outside-In is a business framework and system for creating and sustaining successful organisations. Its central tenet is that all organisations should be built and designed 'Outside-In' with a focus to achieving Successful Customer Outcomes. In industry and business no one invents anything completely new. Rather people see how existing ideas fit into new frameworks. The components of a new idea are usually floating around in the milieu of business research and discourse prior to its discovery.

What is new is the packaging of these components into a cohesive whole. Similarly the idea that all business should be oriented to achieve Successful Customer Outcomes and 'Outside-In' is not entirely new. It has been floating around in various forms for some time. But it is only now assuming its rightful position at the centre of business theory and practice.

Ironically some of the pioneers, both business leaders and theorists, of 'Outside-In' thinking and practice had a notion of how best to align businesses to achieve success. In 1985 Paul Strassman in *'Information Payoff The Transformation of Work in the Information Age'*[ii] discussed how information technology changes the very nature of work and why we do it …. Strassman didn't use the words Successful Customer Outcomes or Outside-In but he was thinking along the same lines.

Since the mid 1980's, terms such as customer centric, Business Process Management and the agile organisation, have grabbed the minds of business leaders and academics alike. They all refer to related ideas. For example, in 1993 Hammer and Champy in their book 'Reengineering the Corporation'[iii] proclaimed the need to 'start over' and rethink the way work is done. Writers and Consultants such as Charles Handy, a leading European authority, academics Kaplan & Norton, author Peter Fingar, Dr. Tom Davenport and many more have written, theorized and in some cases pointed out the pivotal role of the Customer for all organisations.

What has been lacking is putting these disparate ideas into a coherent and practical framework.

This I argue has not been done before and is precisely what Customer Expectation Management Method (CEMMethod[TM]) is all about. While successful 'Outside-In' organisations may not explicitly use the term CEMMethod[TM] the principles, methods and application are there and accessible by others.

> While successful organizations may not explicitly call their approaches 'Outside-In' the principles, methods and application are there and accessible by others.

Some of these success stories include Virgin, South West, BestBuy, FedEx Kinko, Zara plus others and examine emerging best practice and its implications for everyone.

Delivering Successful Customer Outcomes to reduce costs, improve revenue and enhance Service

"Simplicity is the ultimate sophistication" - Leonardo Da Vinci

Competition, globalization, conformance, complexity are all things forcing us to look at how work gets done. To do it better, faster, cheaper.

And boy are we trying. We are looking at efficiency, effectiveness and waste. We monitor the numbers; put them into dashboards and scorecards and....wait.

The language of business seems to be about the battle between companies and customers. What about the phrase 'front line' or 'customer engagement'? Even 'the customer is always right'. They are all confrontational.

Think about how we organize ourselves. If I asked you to sketch your organisation chart what it would look like? Yes, a hierarchical pyramid with the 'big jobs' at the top. Why is that so? It is a mind-set that was created in the Industrial Revolution c. 1770.

An effective strategy for the 21st century?

So why organize ourselves and work in this way?

Because we always have. Now changing times, new and volatile demands are meaning that those ways of doing stuff are just no longer as effective.

Organisations who understand this have already transformed to newer more vitalized business model.

Let's review a couple of examples. Zara, the world's leading fashion retailer take 10 Days from design concept to actually placing merchandise in their stores. This process 'sense and respond' is a seismic shift in performance compared with previous industry norm of 9-12 months..

> "There is only one boss.
> The customer.
> And he can fire everybody in the company from the chairman on down, simply by spending his money somewhere else".
> Sam Walton,
> founder Wal-Mart.

South West Airlines, one of Americas largest passenger airlines, processes start with the customer thinking of a flight to the return home and relaxation. Contrast that with the traditional airlines who share a view of process starting at ticket sale and ending at collecting the bag of the carousel. If your major competitor starts giving away your core revenue earning product for free that is a game changer. For instance South West Airlines are now moving from the 'low cost carrier' to the 'no cost carrier'. There are many fine examples of organisations that have delivered the Outside-In promise and are now going further including Best Buy, Easyjet, Emirates and China Mobile. Later we'll review each of their stories.

So what is the secret, the magic sauce, Colonel Saunders recipe?

The good news – it isn't rocket science. We mere mortals can grasp the fundamentals and make them our own.

It is about organizing ourselves around the person who pays our salary and keeps the shareholders happy – the customer.

Organizing ourselves around the customer reduces cost, improves revenue and enhances service. i.e. The Triple Crown. What's more this is sustainable. In fact it is a new business model. Writers, business gurus and leading practitioners are calling this the Age of Customer Capitalism[iv].

Those folks who don't understand this will be like marooned penguins on a melting iceberg drifting out to sea.

The contrast between the old ways and the new is stark. Ever diminishing returns and a downward spiral for those still looking inside for improvement.

The promise and immediate return in reduced costs, savings and increased revenue for those who understand and apply the new rules of the game.

So how do we do that?

Well for one thing we start where we are – now, today.

We rid ourselves of artificial pictures and boundaries e.g. the pyramidal organisation structure.

We challenge our thinking and ask how does the work I do contribute to achieving our Successful Customer Outcome (SCO)?

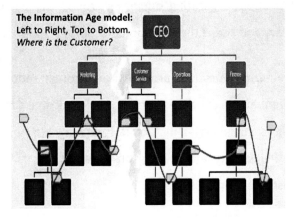

Systematically we need to

1. Work out the needs of those customers you are trying to meet, and understand those needs well.

2. Organize in a clear and simple way around those needs.

3. Articulate those needs as SCOs and align the organisation through its people, processes, systems and strategy

The benefits are immediate and sustainable. Ask yourself the question – what is my unit's Successful Customer Outcome?

How many of our current measures of success are inside-out (old way) and how many Outside-In (new way)?

A real test of current customer alignment – does everybody know (a) the cost of customer acquisition (b) the annual value of a customer (c) the cost of a customer complaint.

> Do you know the current and projected cost of
> Customer Acquisition?
> The Annual Customer Value?
> The cost of a Customer complaint?

It isn't good enough anymore to say it doesn't matter to me, I am in XYZ department and don't need to care. Oh yes you do – and before it is too late!

> "High expectations are the key to everything" – Sam Walton

Organise everything around the Successful Customer Outcome

Organize everything around achieving SCOs and meeting Customer expectations. Progressively review the processes in this light and you will take out cost, improve revenues and enhance service simultaneously.

It is quick, it is simple and it is now.

Zen and the Art of Process Management

Alignment that achieves the Triple Crown

The ultimate success of any commercial business is its ability to generate returns for its shareholders. Achieving healthy and sustained returns requires a deep and broad understanding of customer's needs and wants and the enterprise capability to turn these into profitable services and products. The easiest way to express this requirement in corporate objectives is through Triple Crown capability – the ability to increase revenues, reduce costs and enhance service simultaneously. Inside out organisations however often behave as if these, the ultimate objectives, are mutually exclusive. For instance they mistakenly believe enhancing service increases costs; growing revenue also increases costs. They also believe that when we cut costs service deteriorates. This is a very common misconception particularly in the public sector.

Why does this misunderstanding exist for Inside-out organisations?

We need only look back to the 1970's and 80's which saw a flourishing of Total Quality Management (TQM) and its offspring (still with us – Six Sigma and Lean). Our attention is drawn to the inside-out activities that seemingly contribute to delivering a product or service. We then examine these activities and seek to streamline them and in doing so create an illusion of control and 'process excellence'. This misleading adventure has led many to an ultimate dead-end of diminishing returns and ultimately the search for a new formula, which unfortunately is often an extrapolation of the previous approaches, again destined to fail.

What's required here is a change in perspective, a new way of looking at things and seeing them for what they are. This perspective shows us that fixing effects (what we thought was the process) leads eventually nowhere. We actually need to fix the Causes of Work and in doing so we change *forever* the underlying set of activities that deliver Successful Customer Outcomes. This new process perspective opens our eyes to previously unthought-of possibilities and begins a journey that leads to even greater gains.

South West airlines made this change in perspective resulting in a quantum shift that is evident in their financial results. Initial 'Outside-In' success leads to progressively more gains as the people and company have grown an understanding unrivalled until recently on the US airline industry. Despite the volatility of world markets, terrorism, globalization and the politics of their industry (much of the US airline industry has to be supported by the US tax payer and lurches from one state of bankruptcy to another) South West stand head and shoulder above the crowds with 59 successive quarters of profit in the last 61[v]. Virgin America (VA) are the new kids on the block in the moribund US airline business. Starting from the ground-up (which somehow seems very appropriate for an airline) they have completely designed their enterprise on Outside-In principles, underpinned by Successful Customer Outcomes and Customer Expectation Management. After a difficult birth (the US authorities are lobbied strongly by the existing incumbents) VA emerged to the world in 2007. It is still early days, however already the increased competition on key internal routes is changing the market. As VA expands and knits its hubs with those of Virgin Atlantic and Virgin Pacific the industry changes forever. VA understand the reality of the 21st century - If you are not making your customers lives simpler, easier and more successful your competitors will.

Velocity of Business

Zara have contributed to a sea change in the fashion business. With a dynamic, agile enterprise they have grown from a Spanish

> Zara's 'concept to wear' process takes 10 days against an industry average of 12 months

family owned business in the 1970's to be the world's largest and most successful fashion retailer.

A major contributor to this success has been their understanding of customers *needs* as opposed to customer wants. In a different industry in a different century Henry Ford stated "if we'd have asked the customers what they want they would have said faster horses" and so it is with Zara. Their insight to customer needs has developed a set of processes that can deliver concept to wear in less than 10 days. Compared with an industry average of over nine to 12 months this is a major competitive advantage which brings with it many attributes that make Outside-In thinking and practice so compelling.

> "If I'd have asked customers what they wanted they would have said 'faster horses' ".
> Henry Ford

Those companies that take 12 months to bring clothes to market share a mind-set developed in the Victorian era which says that successful business is complicated; requires sophisticated management approaches; needs logistics and supply chain management; enterprise systems; and reward remuneration systems requiring a degree in Rocket Science to navigate them. All this 'stuff' slows things down and causes problems – ask yourself the question of how many things can go wrong in 12 months? Also how long does it then take to fix them? The cost of putting things right causes these companies to become more risk averse and we now witness the consequences – they are going broke.

Zara on the other hand takes 10 days to achieve a new fashion line. What's the consequence when things go wrong in that time scale? How long does it take to fix it? Accordingly learning and experimentation is a highly prized skillset and with a process velocity of this speed the organisation can change direction overnight to capitalize on emergent trends. In fact Zara have moved to a place where they are actively managing Customer Expectations and in doing so continue to raise the competitive bar even further. This dominance has changed another industry forever and most of us have a whole new bunch of expectations when it comes to buying clothing – we can thank Zara's innovation for that.

Customer Centricity

There are enough hackneyed phrases littering the world of management and business to last us an eternity. Customer Centricity as a term first saw the light of day in the late 1980's during another management brainstorm – Customer Relationship Management (CRM). A software industry developed to automate front-ends and create the automated customer interface, known in the industry as Automated Voice Response Systems (AVRS).

These CRM systems promised to change the way we deal with customers (and unfortunately they have with negative side effects) and along the way become customer centric. It never happened, another promise made of the snake-oil software purveyors which cost lots of money, led to the introduction of short term cost based outsourcing and moved organisations away from the very people they needed to develop intimacy with – you and me, the customer.

The story of AVRS has been a rapid rise and slow decline with smart organisations realising that moving costs out of customer operations just increases cost three or four fold elsewhere. The objective, driven from a functional silo perspective, has been to remove costs and in isolation replacing people with AVRS does precisely that – in the call centre. The remainder of the business operations suffers as a direct consequence and the knock on effect in terms of customer defection has been severe. One notable US company, Cabela's, the world leading outdoor outfitter, saw this sooner than others and acted to put the customer at the centre of everything they do, and within that simple decision scrap all their AVRS's. The company now ensures that every call is answered by a local English speaking person and never by a machine – without exception.

Since its founding in 1961, Cabela's has built its brand on exemplary customer care. This strategy has resulted in tremendous customer loyalty, enabling the company to reach more than $2 billion in sales last year.

The company's culture of service has been widely recognized by independent observers. Business Week, for example,

> At Cabela's every single call is answered by a local English speaking person – no AVRS

ranked Cabela's in its list of the Top 25 Customer Service Elite—making it one of only two retailers (the other being Nordstrom's) to be so honoured. Fast Company named Cabela's one of its 15 "Leading Listeners" and a benchmarking study from Cisco ranked Cabela's #1 among online retailers in customer experience, putting it ahead of such market leaders as Amazon and Best Buy. Ron Spath, VP of Customer Relations says "We don't have any interactive voice recorders and no menus. The feedback we get from our customers is very clear about how they appreciate not having to waste a lot of time talking to a machine. They've also indicated it takes much longer to talk to someone who speaks broken English." Cabela's goes even further, "It's this same line of thinking that leads us to prominently display out toll free number on every page of our Web site. We don't want to frustrate our customers who have questions that they can't find answers to when they visit our Web site."[vi]

So when we talk of customer centricity we do not mean those

isolated islands of automation linked to those intensive call centres full of script following Customer Service Advisors battling call length metrics. The good news is we mean Customer Centricity as pushed by companies such as Cabela's and

Best Buy, Americas leading electronics retailer. The philosophy and practice of putting the customer at the centre of your Universe and making sure that everything is aligned with achieving Successful Customer Outcomes.

Zen and Processes

This is where we can go potentially really freaky. The organisations that are most successful consistently use processes to effectively remove processes. Stay with me... If we acknowledge that much of what we have been doing for the greater part of the last 100 years is fixing effects, and these effects in turn are actually the aggregate of numerous activities that we mostly call processes then applying an Outside-In perspective to these 'processes' achieves something remarkable – the effects disappear as we deal directly with the Causes of Work and what remains is radically simplified.

In reality BP Group and Towers Associates research suggests that more than 60-70% of current work, in traditional organisations is effect based. This opens a massive potential to remove unnecessary activities, speed processes and simultaneously enhance customer service.

To fully understand 'real' process you need to see beyond the place that increasingly proposes complex architectures, taxonomies, and process languages. The world really isn't that complicated, albeit we often seem to make it appear that way.

The former CEO of Citibank, John Reid put this concept very well when articulating what his banking business actually does "We get money in, move it around, and give it out. How difficult do you want to make that?".

Applying our focus to Cause, rather than effect eliminates much of what we think of as process. The golden nugget that remains is indeed our ability to create the Successful Customer Outcome, and as we do so progressively eliminate unnecessary time consuming and costly work.

FedEx applied this thinking to their newly acquired printing operation Kinko (now FedEx Office[vii]) and in doing have changed the business model in their sector forever. By articulating the SCO and making explicit the Causes of Work many Points of Failure have been eradicated. The resulting process bears little resemblance to the starting point and as a direct consequence FedExKinko now lead their sector in terms of volume and profitability.

The Four waves of Process Management

If we take a modern historical perspective we can see four distinct recent waves of process transformation, each wave progressively bringing us greater business benefit (lower costs, growing revenues, improving service and achieving compliance) and improved alignment to customer success.

PERFORMANCE BENEFITS - PROCESS TRANSFORMATION MATRIX
© Towers Associates 2010 – Research 800+companies 2006-2010

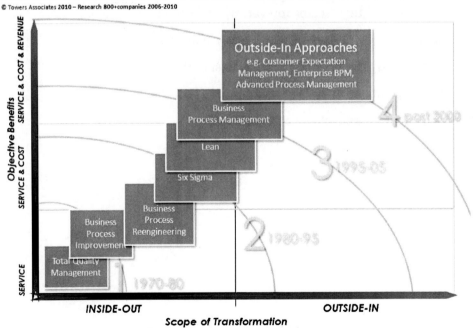

Let's examine each wave of development in turn:

Wave One – Service as a component of performance improvement

Total Quality Management (or TQM) was a management concept coined by W. Edwards Deming. The basis of TQM is to reduce the errors produced during the manufacturing or service process, increase customer satisfaction, streamline supply chain management, aim for modernization of equipment and ensure workers have the highest level of training[viii]. TQM very much put process on the map as the means to achieve these improvements. By examining in detail the processes within departments, objective and measureable improvements, especially in relation to customer service, could be achieved. Unfortunately TQM tended to focus directly on the customer facing processes and achieved little in back office environments which remained hog tied by complexity.

Wave Two – Service & Cost on the agenda

As TQM ran its course three 'new' management approaches gained favour with an increasing drive to improve operational efficiency. The first of these management approaches, Business Process Improvement, brought to the party a range of techniques originally developed by industrial engineers in the post second world war period. The focus on efficiency helped to identify the costs of process, in addition to service improvements. Business Process Improvement tended to emphasize incremental change and while that achieved some success companies facing more severe problems looked further, and enter stage right, Business Process Reengineering (BPR).

The key to BPR was for organisations to look at their business processes from a "clean slate" perspective and determine how they can best construct these processes to improve how they conduct business. Reengineering was a fundamental rethinking and radical redesign of business processes to achieve dramatic improvements in cost, quality, speed, and service. Professor Michael Hammer awakened wide spread interest in BPR with his Harvard Business Review article in 1990 Reengineering Work: Don't automate, obliterate[ix] and for several years BPR sat at the top of the corporate change agenda. By 1995 however the reengineering fervour began to wane as a consequence of poor results and an overly heavy emphasis on cost reduction as the only deliverable. In 1997 the article "What killed BPR"[x] was the final nail in coffin of the approach that burst meteorically onto the scenes and faded just as fast five years later. Early proponents of BPR then collectively shifted their emphasis towards another rapidly emerging approach – Six Sigma.

Six Sigma is a business management strategy originally developed by Motorola, USA in 1981[xi] and became prominent in the mid 1990's as recession focused organisations attention on reducing cost in a less draconian way than BPR.

Six Sigma seeks to improve the quality of process outputs by identifying and removing the causes of defects (errors) and minimizing variability in manufacturing and business processes. It builds on a set of quality and statistical methods, and creates a special infrastructure of people within the organisation ("Black Belts", "Green Belts", etc.) who are supposed experts in these methods. Jack Welch famously claimed his turnaround of General Electric was attributed to the Six Sigma programme. By the late 1990s, about two-thirds of the Fortune 500 organisations had begun Six Sigma initiatives with the aim of reducing costs and improving quality[xii]

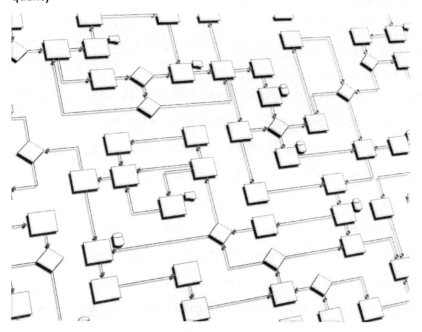

Six Sigma's success has also been part of its decline as the specialist cliques of coloured belts became expensive to maintain and initial cost reduction and service improvements became harder to win. Many adherent companies have struggled to modernise further and many critical articles have resulted in a slow but steady decline in interest in the approach.

The reality is that Six Sigma doesn't extend the organisation scope sufficiently far enough and while it talks of the customer in terms of specification, an over emphasis on 'voice of the customer' and understanding 'customer wants' misses a crucial point in the customer age – it is about understanding and delivering what the customer needs, rather than just seeking to satisfy what the customer says they want.

Wave Three – Service, Cost & Revenue please

The third wave of Process management was heralded by the introduction of Lean manufacturing by Toyota. Toyota's growth from a small car maker to the worlds largest drew attention to the methods and practices developed as a production practice that considers the expenditure of resources for any goal other than the creation of value for the end customer to be wasteful, and thus a target for elimination. To this extent Lean techniques, now including Lean for Service (which de-emphasize the manufacturing component in service companies) moves the agenda much more towards the customer. In more than 80% of cases Lean initiatives[xiii] still look within the organisation, however consideration of external value chains moves the discipline towards the Outside-In perspective.

Lean is renowned for its focus on reduction of the original Toyota *seven wastes*[xiv] to improve overall customer value, but there are varying perspectives on how this is best achieved. Also a focus towards 'value creation' increases the benefit to the organisation beyond just cost reduction and service improvement to include revenue generation as a metric for success. Hybrids of Lean and Six Sigma have developed which seek to bring the best of both disciplines however recent issues with Toyota and 'sticky brakes' have resulted in a trend away from new Lean initiatives.

Even so organisations with an investment in Lean are able to readily embrace more advanced Outside-In approaches, a notable example being PolyOne[xv] (a US Plastics company) that have achieved significant cost reductions, service improvements and revenue generation while at the same time increasing the stock price fivefold in less than six months.

Many would say the natural successor to the earlier process centric approaches is Business Process Management (BPM). The BP Group ran its first BPM training events and seminars in 1993 as a proactive means of building on BPR success.

It is argued that BPM enables organisations to be more efficient, more effective and more capable of change than a functionally focused, traditional hierarchical management approach. In the right hands and in its advanced forms BPM allows organisations to effectively win the 'Triple Crown'. It was Vice President of Gartner Group Jim Sinur who coined 'Triple Crown' in 2004 to explain that by undertaking successfully a BPM program you will, as a by-product simultaneously reduce costs, improve service and grow revenues. BPM also  embraces many of the techniques of earlier approaches however trends since early 2000's indicate a break apart of the management approach into three distinct camps.

- The first camp is technology driven BPM which utilises process modelling and systems to help companies capture processes such as insurance claims and in doing so automate them. As a consequence many people think BPM is a technology solution. As of 2009 Gartner Research recognises 22 companies featuring in their BPM Magic Quadrant analysis.

- The second BPM camp is more a reversion to Business Process Improvement (2nd wave) whereby individual processes are improved within well-defined functional boundaries. This can produce local benefits however inherits a failing of inside-out approaches with potential sub optimization and the presupposition that processes exist to be optimised rather than eradicated. This is largely a scoping issue and reflects the relatively low positioning of BPM in certain companies as a means of improvement rather than a stepping stone to organisation transformation.

- The third camp has evolved BPM to embrace a range of techniques which radically alter the way companies organise their work, and as we see elsewhere rethink their business. The most important aspect of the third camp is an understanding that the only reason a process exists is to contribute to the achievement of Successful Customer Outcomes, otherwise that process is potentially dumb stuff and should be removed.

Wave Four – Service, Cost, Revenue and Customer Expectations – Moving Outside-In

The fourth wave is a confluence of successful approaches that have one thing in common. They are all Outside-In and emphasise the customer as the only reason an organisation exists. This territory currently belongs to the leading global companies who have paved the way for others to emulate their successes by recasting their businesses through the eyes of the customer.

> In doing so Outside-In companies actively select and seek their customers and proactively manage expectations.

Outside-In companies utilise a variety of new techniques that seek to align everything: task, activities, people, systems, and processes to achieving successful customer outcomes. In doing so they actively select and seek their customers and proactively manage those customers expectations.

A clear example of the Outside-In approach is Apple who has grown to dominate their market and after a decade of innovation set the bar for everyone else to jump. Another example, the Virgin group, direct their energy towards delivering customer success through a clear focus on who their customers are, and what skills their people need to meet and exceed customer expectations. In the 2006 book Customer Expectation Management[xvi] we reviewed how Virgin Mobile redefined the US cellular phone sector with this type of innovative Outside-In strategy.

The success of Outside-In is easy to understand and yet many companies have difficulty in moving from functional specialist silo based structures to this new order. Inside-out companies continue to battle complexity and strive to improve efficiencies. In many instances they are busy doing things right but do not understand the rules of the game have changed forever and to paraphrase Deming "you may be doing things right but you need to be doing the right things as well!".

> You may be doing things right, but are you doing the right things?

That is the essence of Outside-In.

Reflections on the State of Play

Pressure to perform has never been greater at both a personal and company level. Each of the approaches has merit depending on the challenge faced however in our recent research increasingly the players who dominate their markets, those achieving triple-crown plus, are utilizing Outside-In approaches and methods.

Common themes to note are these companies 'Outside-In' perspective, their alignment to achieving and exceeding customer expectations, the constant stretch to delivering Successful Customer Outcomes and a relentless focus on business success through reduced costs, improved revenues and enhanced service.

Outside-In is a natural evolutionary approach and yet remarkable in its ability to produce immediate and significant impact on corporate performance. It is readily embraced and incorporates facets of its predecessors. It is easy to understand at all levels (alignment to achieving Successful Customer Outcomes) and does not require significant technology investment.

You may be doing things right, but are you doing the right thing?

As we have discussed the vast majority of techniques, approaches and methods are geared to fixing problems, and essentially getting better at doing things right. That was fine in the 20th century world where efficiency was king. Not so anymore where effectiveness and efficiency are pre-requisites for business success. Just getting better at what you currently do (doing things right) is the route of diminishing returns. The harder we try, the tighter we get, the poorer the gain each time around.

Let's contrast that with doing the right thing. Here we seek to determine what the right thing is, and in our language it centres on Successful Customer Outcomes (SCOs). And that isn't about (just) filling forms correctly, tightening bolts or producing widgets. It is a philosophy that seeks to improve our alignment in everything we do towards the SCO. It is geared to understanding Causes rather than fixing effects, and unfortunately again so much of what is called 'improvement' is about fixing effects, rather than flushing out the Cause of Work (COW) and the Points of Failure (POF).

CEMMethod™

The approach the BP Group have distilled from global leading companies, which we call Customer Expectation Management Method[xvii] CEMMethod™, has a set of principles and philosophy that makes sure everything you do improves the SCO. CEMMethod™ helps an organisation bring their processes, systems, strategy and people into 'Outside-In' alignment.

How does the CEMMethod™ work?

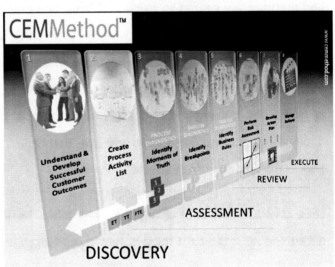

By applying attention to the Causes of Work and fixing those with a rigorous impact assessment, improved ways of working can be collectively discovered and deployed. Organisations using the method readily identify apparently 'dumb stuff' in the context of Outside-In. Stopping this dumb stuff releases cost, improves velocity and enhances control. By applying Outside-In approaches such as CEMMethod™ leading companies are able to create clear water between themselves and the nearest 'inside-out' rivals.

So how could we compare the success of CEMMethod™ with the less effective approaches like Six Sigma and Lean? We can highlight the attributes of each using a simple example:

Six Sigma is about fixing problems and doing things right.

For example people may not be filling in a form correctly. Six Sigma understands how often, where and what could be done to improve accuracy of the form.

> so much of what is called 'improvement' is about fixing effects, rather than flushing out the Cause of Work (COW) and the Points of failure (POF)

Lean is about doing things right, and sometimes doing the right thing.

Lean is similar to Six Sigma however it goes a stage further in removing waste associated within our example of form completion, by removing unnecessary steps and sometimes as a consequence removes the need for a form entirely. In doing so occasionally, but not by design, Lean approaches enable the doing of the right thing.

Both Six Sigma and Lean don't challenge directly whether the example form helps to achieve an SCO.

Outside-In, and the CEMMETHOD™, is about doing the right thing and doing it even Better.

We ask whether the form contributes to the achievement of the SCO. If it doesn't we stop doing this dumb stuff. It is typical to find that large amounts of work are unnecessary, may be stopped and in doing so free up scarce resource.

The good news is that those 'Outside-In' success stories can help all of us embrace the SCO and identify and achieve immediate substantive triple-crown benefits for our organisations.

What is your Successful Customer Outcome and how aligned is your organisation to achieving it?

Successful Customer Outcomes - New Thinking for a New Age

Two items of business news have caught my eye recently: Tesco's latest results, cementing their place as a leading global online retailer and the number one food retailer in the UK; and the start of the latest Stelios venture, easyCruise. Now there may not seem to be much to connect these two organisations but there is, something that is of critical importance to the success of all organisations.

Tesco has been building on its successes for some time now with a relentless commitment to offering what customers want – value, choice, availability. Did you know that Tesco is the world's number one online retailer? You won't find much emphasis on groceries when you listen to Sir Terry Leahy talking about his business. It's about lifestyle. He wants to be able to offer Tesco customers what they want, when and where they want it, at the right price. There's nothing radical in this desire to please, but some organisations are much more successful at this than their rivals.

easyCruise is a fascinating addition to the cruise market. Now this idea may have come from a detailed analysis of the holiday market in general and cruising in particular but I don't think so.

The approach of the easyGroup to date has been to understand what people need and to work out how to do it, even if that means turning industry norms upside down. To many people cruising is expensive, takes up a lot of time, and is quite formal in its style and structure.

For the younger holidaymaker brought up on independent travel, and with the belief that holidaying is a time to let your hair down rather than put it up, cruising doesn't have a lot going for it. Unless you could stay in a port for as long as you liked and pick up the next passing ship when you were ready; and there was clubbing on board; and you could dress how you wanted; and it was cheap.

Bingo. A traditional company might say that that's not cruising. Stelios would say, who cares if it isn't cruising if that is actually what the customers want.

OK so you've probably spotted the link between these stories – commitment to the customer. That's old hat, I hear you say; we all have that. But the truth is that most organisations are not doing this at all well. So is there something we can distil from the companies that are doing it right? In many cases the successful organisations have stumbled on ways of working that help them to do what they want to do. There is no obvious pattern that can be repeated at will in any business, so I believe that we have to look at behaviours - behaviours that can be absorbed and translated into the sort of focus that can transform a business.

Another organisation that has been able to forge real success from a commitment to customers is Capital One. A rapidly growing financial services company, Capital One tells a very good story about how it has transformed an already successful business - their case study is an article in its own right. The key points will give some sense of what the management there have learned:

> • an analysis of the business showed that they were doing things right, and they were making continuous efforts to improve. They characterize this perspective as being an "inside-out" view of their own organisation;

• the turning point came when they took a customer view ("Outside-In") of how they did business. They realised that they could do more of the right things. This meant a move away from traditional performance measures such as call volumes, processing times and basic customer satisfaction;

• in their place Capital One started to measure the revenue being added, cost reductions achieved and service improvements for customers;

• Crucially it was these measures that determined how staff would be rewarded.

Even in a short summary of what is a fascinating case study we can see some of the challenges that organisations face in transforming how they do business, and I will come to those a little later. I want to look first at the changes that Capital One made and why I think they are so important.

Capital One was doing very well by measuring activity and improving performance where possible. The real leap was made was when

> ... link staff rewards directly to Successful Customer Outcomes

they started to measure the impact of Successful Customer Outcomes (SCOs). Not only did they measure SCOs, they linked staff rewards directly to SCO delivery. This is the only way to embed changed behaviours in an organisation. If you can link behaviours to your objectives and drive the right behaviours through your reward system then you can achieve pretty much whatever you want.

So the big question to go and ask the senior people in any organisation is: how are you rewarded for what you do? The vast majority will have a system whereby rewards are linked to the successful delivery of a range of tasks and activities based on the corporate objectives. Until now this sounded like the right answer, but it's fundamentally flawed. The introduction of SCOs as a measure of real customer-oriented performance will cut across many of these task-led objectives and therefore the reward system. Any company trying to operate like this will never achieve what it is trying to do.

Here's another example. Let's compare how a traditional major airline and, say, easyJet approach corporate objectives and performance measures. A major airline looks to deliver a quality air transport service, cost effectively. This translates into a bunch of objectives which are cascaded through the hierarchical structure via performance targets and associated rewards. At easyJet, from the top man down, the focus is on putting bums on seats. So everyone can ask themselves every day, what am I doing to get more bums on seats? And they will ask that, because a large chunk of their salary is dependent on it.

> easyJet's focus is putting 'Bums on Seats'

If you work in an organisation that has aligned itself to Successful Customer Outcomes and 40% of your pay is linked to delivering them, then you will absolutely want to deliver them. And the first question you will ask? What the heck are our successful customer outcomes?

Good management will give you the answers clearly, and before you know it everyone is lined up behind clear customer-related objectives - focused and motivated. In this context initiatives like CRM implementations stop being islands of technology and become widely appreciated tools for helping deliver performance and rewards.

Now let's come back to the big problems facing many businesses as they gear up to the challenge of aligning themselves to SCOs. To do this we need to run through a potted history of organised work. Simplifying this enormous subject a little, I'll just talk about the key periods, or ages. Firstly there was the Agrarian age, farming based on individual labour. This was followed by the Industrial age where mechanisation and large scale organisation took over.

> The difficulty lies not in the New Ideas, but in escaping the old ones
>
> John Maynard Keynes

More recently we have seen the Information age emerge quickly,

promising rapid change across many industries. This heritage of working methods explains why we work the way we do now. Hierarchies evolved to meet the challenge of organising large numbers of people carrying out set tasks and activities. The "management pyramid" underpins many of today's working practices, our understanding of how to make labour efficient, and most theories about leadership. It has served us well but the world is changing, driven by globalization, and as customers we have quite a different set of requirements now.

The challenge for organisations is to be more agile, flexible, and responsive to these changing customer needs. Companies across the world have indulged in restructuring that has focused on moving chairs around, while avoiding the issue that the structures they are trying to apply aren't fit for purpose in the new world.

And this new world isn't limited to the much discussed corporate/customer relationship: the provision of public services to citizens, all business to business activity, in fact every relationship between people and organisations is in need of an overhaul.

John Maynard Keynes (English economist, journalist, and financier) once said "The difficulty lies, not in the new ideas, but in escaping from the old ones"[xviii]. This quote may be decades old but it has real resonance today.

Out-dated mind-sets are the single biggest obstacle to an organisation's ability to align to Successful Customer Outcomes. In the same way that the early Information age companies clung for too long to an Industrial age view of doing business, with their organized banks of computers set out like factory spaces, today's organisations are clinging to the rigid hierarchies that were needed to make Industrial age production operations work.

The need to reassess and fundamentally realign structures and priorities is paramount – any organisation that can't make the leap must face the prospect of being left behind in this new age.

Screw it. Let's do it. Take Process to the Next level.

There are those people who believe that for anything to be successful it must be difficult and complex. I was reminded of this when reading some recent reviews of Richard Bransons excellent short read - *Screw it - Let's Do it*[xix] when apparently well-educated and experienced people dissed the book because it was' too simple' and childish. Wake up and smell the coffee! We have collectively through the industrial and Information Age surrounded ourselves with rules (the vast majority now out dated) and red tape born of a time when  customers didn't have choice and the work world was dominated by hierarchy and control.

Bransons writing is a breath of fresh air as he shares with us the trials and tribulations of creating one of the 21st century's major success stories with over 200 global companies heading-up their respective business sectors.

For those inside out thinkers the message of simplicity and customer focus is akin to the medieval flat landers hearing the world was round, collectively burying their heads in the sand hoping the truth just might go away. Unfortunately some people just don't get the New World.

I am reminded of the remark John Corr, Director at Alix Partners, one of the worlds leading M&A specialists, once told me that it's going to take 25 years for organisations to align to customer success. When I asked why is it going to take so long he replied ".. it will take 25 years for these inside-out flat land Directors to die!"

The good news is of course we have passed the tipping point and the rapid demise of several previously respected names is testament to rise of the new bloods that play the game by a different set of rules centred

> "Knowing the right thing and not doing it is the ultimate cowardice"
> Confucius

around Successful Customer Outcomes (SCO's). We'll discuss and review the successful strategy and tactics shortly however first let's just remind ourselves of some really dumb things those inside-out guys carry on doing:

Dumb stuff the Inside-Outers do to make our lives difficult

Those Restaurants - that charge extra for more than six people in one booking. How does that work? So we reduce the kitchen to and fro. We pay with one payment. We vacate the table at the same time. We make the chef's life easier. We bring more revenue than several tables with 2-3 people. There's more but you get the picture.

Taxis - (especially the ones in Washington DC) that have such complex charging structures (84 different options within a 10 mile radius) each driver needs a special calculator, and still can't get it right. It's a nightmare for the customer, driver, cab firm and the tax man (boy it must be bad to get sympathy there!)

The American Airline - who make people with lots of air miles second class citizens and demote them to the back of the queue, even if you do have the super dooper global travel platinum membership.

The Retail Chain Store - who ask you to return goods to where you bought them (even though they are a global brand with retail outlets everywhere) and then when you do they give you a 'credit' rather than a refund and act as if you are inconveniencing them.

A Car Hire Company - who, despite already having all your details electronically and have you as a member with a 'Five Star Excellency Most Exulted Prized Presidential Customer' level hand you off between front desk, back office window, driver allocator and then boy racers seemingly intent on running you down. They have also persistently tried to sell you upgrades you don't need and provide you with GPS systems that don't work.

And these examples extend into our 'business to business' lives big time with, for example, silly invoicing rules (have you seen what you need to provide for one certain ERP systems company?), red tape and incredibly complex ways of doing relatively simple things.

So how can you avoid these disasters from either the receiving or giving perspective? I have distilled a Top ten list based on BP Group (www.bpgroup.org) research with over 800 organisations. Also remarkably the distribution of businesses shows that companies are doing all or very little, and that goes a long way to explain why successful companies continue to create clear water between themselves and their rivals.

One industry offers striking evidence with 2008 Q1 results including:
Figure 1 - US Airlines Profitability Q1 2008

Delta	$6.4 Billion Loss
Northwest Airlines	$4.1 Billion Loss
Continental	$80 Million Loss
United	$54 Million Loss
Southwest	$14 Million Profit

And what's next? The two airlines suffering the most merged - Delta and NWA. I suppose the thinking there might be an economy of scale where they would only lose half as much?

Southwest, now the 2nd biggest carrier of people in the US[xx], and with 59 of the last 61 quarters profitable, achieves this consistent success by ensuring everything reinforces Successful Customer Outcomes including actions such as 'buying long' (purchasing fuel at fixed prices), understanding where the real customer process starts and finishes and progressively extending the value chain to include items other than just seat sales.

For every dumb inside-out example there's now a rival, usually leading the pack who like Southwest Airlines are so Outside-In focused that they are more than profitable. They crush the competition with an ability to reduce costs and improve service simultaneously. So what are the lessons we can learn from the leaders?

The 'How To' Top Ten List to Achieve Outside-In Capability

1. ### Define your Customer

   A couple of kick starters here include asking the organisation 'what business are we in?' and 'who is the person/group/company that provides us with revenue?'
   Too often organisations create a mass of so called internal customers and the resulting customer-supplier internal relationships do not contribute to achieving a Successful Customer Outcome for the real customer.

2. Articulate your Successful Customer Outcome (SCO)

Hallmark Cards, now in its second century, based in the US out of Kansas City define their SCO as "Expression". A pharmaceutical company define theirs as "healthy lifestyle" and a religious organisation "bringing people to God". A good SCO will catapult performance as people better understand how their contribution adds to the achievement of the SCO.

3. Establish your alignment to achieving the SCO

Four areas to start from include people reward systems, systems capability, process maturity and strategic endeavour. If you have a Scorecard or Strategy map ask yourself how many performance measures (a) contribute to the SCO, and (b) are forward looking to progressively help us get better at delivering results. We can't go forward by just looking in the rear view mirror.

4. Identify customer touch points - Moments of Truth (MOT)

Customers are the Cause of Work. Every interaction we have with them results in work for our organisation and creates Points of Failure. Apple have done a phenomenal job in bringing the iPhone and iPad to market and integrating the MOTs into a slick interface. Rather than many key presses for a simple operation like getting the contact list those various actions have been combined into one finger swiping Moment of Truth and in doing so made the customers life simpler, easier and more successful. Once you have identified the MOTs the edict is 'remove or improve'

5. Reveal internal hand-offs - Breakpoints (BP)

Moments of Truth spawn Breakpoints. Every customer interaction requires us to go away and do stuff internally. The resulting activity with hand-offs between departments, people, systems and functions are Breakpoints. These Points of Failure result in unnecessary non value added work which from recent BP Group Research may be as much as 70-90% of what actually goes on in a company. Once identified Breakpoints should be removed.

6. Capture the Business Rules (BR)

Business Rules determine our behaviour. They tell us what to do and when. Frequently BR's were created to prevent things going wrong and get forgotten as we change and develop our businesses. Identify them, make them explicit and challenge them.

Figure 6: Process Activity Map with Moments of Truth, Breakpoints and Business Rules documented

7. Perform an Impact and Risk Assessment against Customer Needs

Are you delivering what the customer says they want, or actually what they really need? Henry Ford said "If I'd have asked customers what they wanted they would have said 'faster horses' ". Are you creating the equivalent of faster horses and then wondering why sales are struggling? Do your processes rely on input from self-selecting customers analysed by the marketing teams? Get the real customer in there. Seek the answers and then match the real need.

8. **Develop an Outside-In Action Plan**

   Many of the inside-out plans are really more about dealing with symptoms and effects rather than the true Causes of Work. Truly Outside-In Action Plans are about reinforcing the achievement of SCO's through process change and subsequently defining and managing new customer expectations. How many of us knew we needed an Apple iPhone before they were invented? What about that extra fancy drink from Starbucks that you are addicted to? What about the personal loan that hits your bank account the same day?

9. **Execute the Plan as you go (simple and no nonsense)**

   Many plans stay exactly that - just plans. The Outside-In reality demonstrates that many actions revolve around stopping the dumb stuff which shouldn't need escalated sign-offs and committees to push them through. One recent survey suggested that more than 80% of the effort around plans in inside-out organisations consisted of talking about, getting buy-in and then achieving sign-off. If you are doing dumb stuff then stop it. Now.

10. Begin the Journey to the Outside-In world now.

Waiting for executive sign-off or consensus will never get you off the launch pad. There's that old Irish joke of when you are lost in Eire and you stop to ask a guy directions and he ponders, stares off into space for a couple of minutes and then offers the sage wisdom "I wouldn't start from here". Most of us don't have a choice - just get started. Examine everything you do from the Outside-In perspective and begin where ever you are currently to implement this 'call to arms'. Your progress as individuals, teams or improvement initiatives will get noticed soon because you will be achieving Triple Crown success - taking out costs, improving service, and ultimately driving more revenue to the bottom line.

"...keep things simple. People get lost when a systematic approach becomes over complex and they lose sight of the actual goal." Richard Branson[xxi].

In doing so you will be creating a sustainable, agile and responsive enterprise where everyone explicitly contributes to individual, team and corporate success.

The Enlightened Customer

The 21st century is indeed a very different place and to best explain that we are going to review the size and scope of these changes.

Customer Promiscuity

A senior Director at Capital One bank observed in 2005 "The customer is the biggest problem," which of course is a typical proclamation for the overworked executives in many organisations, however this time the sarcasm led to a more incisive analysis. He continued "what the customer doesn't realise is how much we invest in running campaigns like 0% interest deals for six months. All the marketing, sales and infrastructure with people and systems is very expensive, so much so that it typically takes nearly 18 months to Break-even on those new customers."

Isn't that the cost of winning new business? Well quite, and in the last century there was money to be made as we could lock customers to our service with penalty charges and admin fees if they moved their business elsewhere. This is no longer the case. Customers move with the times and demand greater flexibility so banks are not able to attract customers when their products have a ball and chain attached. He added, "and do you know what customers do when the 0% rate expires? Yes, they move their business somewhere else! These days the customers have become promiscuous - they will go with anyone."

What about your own buying preferences? Do you vary where you shop, where you spend your vacation, which restaurants you eat at? In the majority of cases we all do. Businesses that deal with customers were not designed with this volatility and promiscuity in mind.

Customer Expectations

Peter Fingar[xxii] says "Seemingly simple ideas are often the most powerful, and the hardest to uncover. In the 20th century, it was Peter Druckers Management by Objectives. In the 21st  century, it's Management by Expectation. This simple, yet powerful, idea of defining your business, not in terms of the goods and services you provide, but in terms of Customer Expectations." Why is this so? The customer experience when we purchase a product or service establishes a future expectation. If things go well our expectations may be high the next time round. Companies who understand the customer experience is shaped by process can gain control over that experience and in doing so *manage future expectations.*

Fingar continues "Linking corporate strategy down into every niche and corner of the enterprise to ensure that your business sets and meets customer expectations." Leading companies such as Zara understand the strategic imperative of creating and managing expectations. In doing so they lift the competitive bar and further reinforce 'good' customer experience. Also once expectations are set they do not revert to a lower level, for instance, flying Virgin Atlantic. The customer experience is usually a great one. We come to expect it. Then we fly British Airways (BA) to be met by surly staff who seem to think customers are an inconvenience to a good flight. Why can't BA be as good as Virgin? It directly influences our purchase decision the next time, and the next.

Managing customer expectations allows companies to increase the customer pipeline, convert higher percentages of that pipeline to profitability, and extend the duration of the customer relationship where profitability is at its peak. As price differentials narrow and product

> "...Customer Expectation Management should figure high on the corporate agenda – it is an operational and strategic imperative"

features are quickly copied, business survival requires an unrelenting focus upon identifying and delivering additional and differentiating value for customers.

Customer Expectation Management should figure high on the corporate agenda – it is an operational and strategic imperative.

Customer Choice

Lloyds TSB, a UK bank had two channels to market (postal, branch), five products and two main processes (sales and service) in 1975[xxiii]. Thirty years later the business had grown to five channels, thirty plus products and seven core processes and yet still manages its business in much the same way. This growth in functionality was a direct consequence of customer pressure, driven through competitor offerings and the need to compete against similar increasingly complex financial service companies. The range of choice demanded by customers whether they are B2C or B2B increases every day and yet the response to providing that choice relies on structures created when the world was a simpler place. Customer choice places a great stress on organisations to offer flexibility and immediate service against a backdrop of fierce competition, increasing regulation and customer promiscuity.

Multiple Channels, Multiple Tiers

"I want to do business my way" has become a customer demand in recent years. The advent of the web, globalisation, in the moment demand, price and localisation insist that companies sell both through multiple channels e.g. off the page, mail, footfall retail, online, social community, and to multiple tiers of

> "...keep things simple. People get lost when a systematic approach becomes over complex and they lose sight of the actual goal."
> Richard Branson

customers. Selling directly to customers is the simplest approach however even that has many alternative 'routes to market'. If you are, for instance, a Novartis drug rep you will be selling prescription medicines to physicians and hospitals. These medicines are prescribed to patients, who in turn go to the drug store that dispenses the prescriptions. There may be many layers of middlemen in the distribution system. In the middle of this complexity lives many customer-supplier relationships all leading to the ultimate revenue generator for the total value chain, the consumer. This is a completely different prescription then when Novartis started as Geigy back in 1758 in Basle, Switzerland.

Prosumer

When you are choosing a product what research do you do? Before you visit the store or shop online it is more than likely you will check the web and the previous buyers. You get yourself informed and review the options and may well access dedicated communities appropriate to your purchase. There is a 'wisdom of crowds' (to quote best-selling author James Surowiecki) and a trust and faith in people you have never met who share your same interests. So if you are buying a book look no further than Amazon.com.

If you intend staying at a hotel visit TripAdvisor.com. In essence you will then trust Martin from Albuquerque, New Mexico than a previously so called authoritative source such as the travel press or New York Times. More than that as a Prosumer you will probably know more about the product you are buying than the people who are actually selling it to you. Apple understand the Prosumer and offer a totally different experience in their world-wide stores. Have you sampled that

> "Customer Enlightenment is a radical departure from the past and is the new normal."

process and observed how radically different that is from a typical retail experience? The Prosumer is a new breed of animal, informed, articulate and incredibly particular.

Customer Rebellion

Making a sale is comparatively easy. When customers are treated with respect and looked after the revenues generated from repeat business will far exceed the original order. However when customers are treated badly, or simply ignored they don't come back and more  must be spent to win new customers. This point is made clear when we contrast shoppers of the 1960's with todays consumer. Fifty years ago shoppers tended to be loyal to the neighbourhood and shops were run by individuals, often family friends in the local community. As a consequence retailers only put 1% of their revenue into sales and marketing. The advertisements were about telling shoppers about new arrivals.

Todays retailers budget between 9-12% for advertising and yet customers don't believe the adverts "Anyone can say that about themselves, I don't believe it." That is one aspect of the rebellion, the other is ensuring service meets high expectations as otherwise the promiscuous customer will vote with their feet. An America Research Group Study in 2008 showed that 63% of new car owners do not go back to the same dealership to buy their next car and the only way to improve that number is to provide exceptional service all the time. At the same time your competitors strive for their own exceptional customer offering.

Customer Enlightenment is a radical departure from the past and is the new normal. The old rules just don't apply anymore and we need to move our organisations to a new place of understanding, a new way of doing business. That way we call Outside-In

The Causes of Work

Fixing effects is a lot like shuffling the chairs on the deck of the Titanic. Lots of work gets done and things look different but the original problem still remains.

Fixing effects increases the complexity of our work and the technology we use to support it. It's a vicious cycle many of us are stuck in. The more we do the worse it gets. Soon analysis paralysis sets in. We're stuck and there's no place for us to go.

Meanwhile successful companies around the world are now eliminating causes rather than fixing effects. But how do they spot causes and eliminate them? Is a host of Master Black Belt Cause Eliminators needed to get the job done?

Of course not. Moments of Truth, Break Points and Business Rules are the causes of work. Once we start looking for them we spot them. Elimination comes from challenging what we currently do - looking for Actions that eliminate Moments of Truth, Break Points and Business Rules.

As discussed earlier every Customer Interaction is a Moment of Truth (MOT). Whether it's person to person, person to system, system to person, system to system or person to product they are all Causes of Work.

This work in dealing with MOT's creates internal handoffs, these are Breakpoints. Places where things can and do go wrong and we see them happening between people, systems and services all the time.

"... Moment of Truth is an insight that 25 years later separates the winners from the losers"

All our internal communications are in fact Breakpoints. For instance how many emails do you receive from colleagues and business partners daily? How many calls do you have to make to get the job done? How many 'systems' do you work with?

A study conducted by researchers at the Universities of Glasgow and Paisley in Scotland found that one third of users felt overloaded and stressed by the heavy volume of e-mail they had to deal with.

When e-mail behaviour was tracked it was found that many were checking their inbox as often as 30 to 40 times per hour. "There was a mismatch between how often people thought they looked at their inbox and how often they actually did it," said Mario Hare, a lecturer at the University of Paisley[xxiv].

With those facts in mind Intel has become the latest in an increasingly long line of companies to launch a so-called 'no e-mail day'.

On Fridays, 150 of its engineers revert to more old-fashioned means of communication. Engineers are encouraged to talk to each other face to face or pick up the phone rather than rely on e-mail. In Intel's case the push to examine breakpoints followed a comment from chief executive Paul Otellini criticising engineers "who sit two cubicles apart sending an email rather than get up and talk".

Energy-draining monster

Obviously switching e-mail off is not the answer to stress and lack of productivity in the office. We really need to get to grips with the Causes of Work – the Moments of Truth and begin to engineer those away. Back in the 1970's Richard Normann[xxv], a renowned Swedish management guru, identified that a major Cause of Work for any organisation is the customer interaction, or Moment of Truth as he termed. That phrase was then immortalized by Jan Carlzon, President of Scandinavian Airlines (SAS), who wrote the book Moments of Truth (1986)[xxvi] capturing his story of the turnaround in fortunes of SAS. His observation that by rationalising the Moments of Truth you could significantly reduce wasteful activity is an insight that 25 years later separates business winners from the also-rans.

Alan Elliot, director of business development of e-mail specialists Mirapoint agrees and says "Depicting e-mail as some kind of resource-draining monster that we'd all be better off without wilfully ignores the realities of the modern business world."[xxvii]

By truly fixing the Causes of Work, rather than messing around with the Effects (a bit like moving the chairs on the deck of the Titanic) we will all find our customers and employees life simpler, easier and more successful.

So how many Causes of Work have you eradicated today?

A New Order of Things Outside-In. Your immediate first steps

There is no easy way to introduce a new order of things however there are some principles that can be followed based on this type of mind shift.

1. Objective and immediate.

The results we achieve with Outside-In are significant and substantive. Accordingly any effort should first of all identify the clear tangible benefits.

2. Talk is cheap.

Fine words and phrases will not win hearts and minds without substance. Delivery is key, hence the 'start where you are' sentiment. In current projects (where

> By fixing the Cause you remove the Effect.

support may be lacking) introduce the techniques within the CEMMethod™ by stealth.

Lift the heads of those around you to think of Moments of Truth, Break Points and Business Rules for instance. You can introduce

Outside-In with stealth, for instance one line a colleague used when faced with the daunting sight of 2,000 green-belted Six Sigma practitioners was "Nothing new, just some stuff other guys have used within their initiative to take their process excellence to a new level." For 'process excellence' substitute your organisations particular flavour of old style process/performance improvement.

3. Build support.

With (2) underway you will build support. That is the point to shift focus and begin the more practical discussion of where and how. By delivering results, if necessary even on a small scale, you will draw attention to your projects delivering results way beyond 'normal' expectations. This groundwork provides an excellent base to begin the real work of organisation transformation.

4. Go for broke.

If you are extremely persuasive and have the top team already on-board go for broke. Discover the worst most problematic issues and set to righting them.
A good place to look is the strategy as that will usually identify the key challenges and opportunities for the business within various timescales. By understanding where those challenges touch the

> "We are at that very point in time when a 400-year-old age is dying and another is struggling to be born – a shifting of culture, science, society and institutions enormously greater than the world has ever experienced.
>
> Dee Hock

organisation you can readily help with the tools and techniques that aid delivery of Outside-In. If you are focused and identify some early deliverables, especially with a view to reducing the amount of unnecessary work in current processes you will quickly win hearts and minds. Your immediate successes will build and lead to broader scale opportunities. Very quickly you will be working with the core organisation processes.

By fixing the Cause you will remove the Effect.

5. Move on.

It is a 400 year shift in mind-set (Dee Hock, VISA founder). It will ultimately transform the planet. The jury is in fact back and the results speak for themselves. So when all looks desolate and casting your pearls before swine is depressing, remind them that they are part of the problem and move on. That can be within your immediate team or department. It is unlikely to be at the organisational level as the logic of Outside-In is persuasive to those people seeking to significantly reduce costs, enhance service and grow revenues.

Those guys will become advocates and want more.

6. Make it so.

You are not alone, it just feels that way when surrounded by flat-landers. Learn, exchange and do. Within your business identify the like-minded, develop a support group, and grow a centre of excellence. Share stories, exchange results and meet with your peers in other companies.

The BP Group community is designed for just that.

The Four ways we can transform processes forever

Traditional process thinking has applied itself to the organisation tasks and activities that constitute what is defined as a process.

Through techniques and methods such as Lean, Six Sigma and Process Management businesses have focused attention on reducing elapsed times, improving efficiency and removing non value added activity.

1. Understand and apply Process diagnostics
2. Identify and align to Successful Customer Outcomes
3. Reframe process for an Outside-In world
4. Rethink the business you are in

These improvements are welcome however often struggle in maintaining on-going gains and unfortunately initial results are often eroded requiring a subsequent revisit and further work to 'maintain' the same processes. This 'Hawthorne effect'[xxviii] is created as a consequence of the thinking and assumptions made when these techniques are applied and comes from a misunderstanding of what process is.

In a manufacturing context, such as a car production line, we can see the process, we can touch it, and it is very tangible in nature. It physically exists and accordingly the process diagrams can be precisely accurate. The vast majority of processes are not in manufacturing – they are service processes and represent everything else that isn't a production line.

In an airline the atmosphere, the attitude and the feelings that are part of the whole experience are intangible, but are critical aspects of the service. How you are treated in a restaurant, how you are treated on an airline - these are all important parts of the service delivery, which is part of the customer experience. The nature of the two types of process is typically not clearly understood and tools suited to manufacturing are incorrectly applied to service processes.

Ask ten people to observe a manufacturing process and you should see an analysis which has 95% solid agreement. Ask the same ten to observe a service process and you will be challenged to achieve any consensus on what is actually happening.

> We force fit service process to adhere to a standard which presents an illusion of 'production line' rigour.
>
> "It is like trying to eat soup with a steak knife"

Even so 'trying harder' means forcing an agreement with such things as 'As Is' analysis during the course of which seeking to agree can take weeks and months, at the end of which the process is still no more real. An additional challenge presents when seeking further agreement around service processes with techniques such as business process modelling language. We force fit service process to adhere to a standard which presents an illusion of 'production line' rigour. In the face of this misapplied thinking John Corr, Director at Alix Partners, commented "It is like trying to eat soup with a steak knife". Accordingly we need a fresh look at what actually causes processes to be this way and that is the essence of what we see successful customer oriented companies doing and we call this 'Outside-In'.

For companies pursuing Outside-In there are several innovative ways to dramatically improve performance through process. These performance improvements demonstrate significant and often double digit deliverables across cost reduction, service improvement and revenue generation. They are reviewed and applied in full within the CEMMethod™ however here we present an overview and broadly categorise them as follows:.

1. Understand and apply Process diagnostics
2. Identify and align to Successful Customer Outcomes
3. Reframe process for an Outside-In world
4. Rethink the business you are in

1: Understand and Apply Process Diagnostics

Earlier we have mentioned Moments of Truth, those all-important interactions with customers. Let's take that discussion further and include other closely related techniques for uncovering the real nature of process – breakpoints and business rules.

Moments of Truth

We have mentioned Moments of truth earlier however let's dig deeper and see how they can be used as a resource to help understand and fix the Causes of Work. To reiterate Moments of Truth (MOT) were first identified by Swedish management guru Richard Normann (1946-2003) in his doctoral thesis "Management and Statesmanship" (1975). In 1989 Jan Carlzon, the CEO of Scandinavian Airlines (SAS) immortalized the phrase with his book 'Moments of Truth'. Carlzon clearly linked all customer interaction as the Causes of Work for the airline and set about eradicating non value added MOT's and then improving those he couldn't remove.

> Moments of Truth should be eradicated. The customer experience improves, costs are reduced and productivity maximised

   a) Moments of Truth are a Process Diagnostic
   b) They occur ANYWHERE a customer "touches" a process

   c)   They can be person-to-person, person-to-system, systems-to-person, system-to-system, and person-to-product

   d)   ANY interaction with a customer is a Moment of Truth

   e)   Moments of Truth are both process Points of Failure and Causes of Work

Carlzon transformed the fortunes of SAS with this straightforward insight – all work in our organisation is ultimately caused by the Moment of Truth. Fix them and you fix everything else.

All Moments of Truth should be eradicated and those remaining improved. In doing so the customer experience is improved, costs are reduced and productivity maximised.

Breakpoints

Next let's review Breakpoints. Breakpoints (BP's) are the direct consequence of MOT's and are all the internal interactions that take place as we manage the processes caused by the customer interactions.

   a) Any place that a hand-off occurs in the process is a Break Point

   b) Break Points can be person to person, person to system, system to person or system to system

   c) Break Points are both process Points of Failure and Causes of Work

By identifying BP's we can set about uncovering actions that would in turn remove them, or if not improve them. BP's are especially evident where internal customer supplier relationships have been established say between Information Systems departments and Operations. Empirical research suggests that for every Moment of Truth there are an average of 3 to 4 Breakpoints. In other words a process with ten MOT's will typically yield 30-40 Breakpoints.

> All Breakpoints should be eradicated. If they cannot be removed they must at the very least be improved.

All Breakpoints should be eradicated and if not at the very least improved. In doing so we get more done with less, red tape is reduced, control improves and the cost of work comes down.

Business Rules

The third in our triad of useful Outside-In techniques is Business Rules. Business Rules are points within a process where decisions are made.

a) Any decision point in a process is a Business Rule
b) Some Business Rules are obvious while others must be "found"
c) Business Rules can be operational, strategic or regulatory and they can be system-based or manual
d) Business Rules control the "behavior" of the process and shape the "experience" of those who touch it

> Business Rules should be challenged in todays context and removed if no longer relevant.

e) Business Rules are highly prone to obsolescence
f) We must find and make explicit the Business Rules in the process

Business Rules (BR's) are especially pernicious in that they are created for specific reasons however over time their origin is forgotten but their impact remains. For instance one Life insurance company had a delay of eight days before issuing a policy once all the underwriting work was complete. This has a serious impact on competitiveness as newcomers were able to issue policies in days rather than weeks.

After some investigation it was discovered that the '8 day storage' rule was related to the length of time it takes ink to dry on parchment paper. This rule hadn't surfaced until the customer expectations changed. There are many examples of previously useful rules evading new 21st century logic and blocking the achievement of successful customer outcomes.

All Business Rules should be made explicit and challenged in today's context.

2: Identify and align to Successful Customer Outcomes

As a guiding principle the only reason an organisation exists is to provide product or service to a customer, as through this mechanism we create the value that pays the stockholders, or in non-profits e.g. civil service, meets the citizen/consumer requirements. Accordingly it stands to reason that all organisations should endeavour to achieve successful customer outcomes (SCO's). For Outside-In companies it is a matter of course that everything within a process is evaluated against this criteria "is this piece of work contributing to the SCO?".

> "Businesses can be very sloppy about deciding which customers to seek out and acquire"
>
> Frederick F. Reichheld

If it isn't contributing then it is potentially 'dumb stuff' in today's context and can be removed. So if SCO's are so important how can we create and subsequently manage them?

A rational way to uncover the SCO is using the SCO Map technique. Through a drill down process it seeks to identify the true customer need, rather than the perceived 'want'. The SCO Map objective is to clearly articulate the need and produce a set of key performance indicators that measure our ability to meet this need. The SCO extends way beyond legacy inside-out thinking to create an actionable strategic and operational objective for the entire organisation.

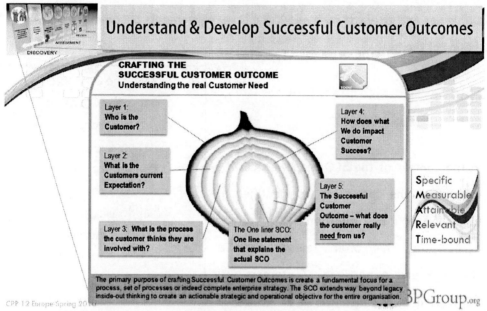

The six questions we ask ourselves in this iterative process are:

Layer 1: Who is the customer?

At first glance this should be an easy answer however it is not as obvious as it seems. The ultimate customer for any profit making enterprise is the person, or company who provides the revenue by purchasing the products or services we produce. It is a matter of fact that in our inside-out legacy world we have created multiple customer-supplier relationships which include internal 'service' providers such as Information Services, Human Resources and so on. In mature Outside-In organisations the internal customer ceases to exist as we progressively partner to align to Successful Customer Outcomes and artefacts such as Service Level Agreements becoming a thing of the past.

Layer 2: What is the Customers current expectation?

In the context of the SCO map we need to understand the customers (as identified in the answer to question 1) current expectation. This often reveals both a challenge and opportunity. Customers will tell it as it is, for instance in an insurance claim process "I expect it is going to take weeks, with lots of paperwork and many phone calls". That should tell you the current service is most likely poor and fraught with

> 1. Who is the Customer?
> 2. What is the Customer's current expectation?
> 3. What process does the customer think they are involved with?
> 4. What do we do that Impacts Customer Success?
> 5. The Successful Customer Outcomes – what does the customer really need from us
> 6. What is the one line statement that best articulates our Successful Customer Outcome?

problems, delays and expensive to manage however this presents the opportunity. If that is a market condition (all insurance claims are like this) then moving to a new service proposition will be a potential competitive differentiator.

Layer 3: What process does the customer think they are involved with?

In the inside-out world we see process in a functional context. Therefore insurance claims are dealt with by an insurance claims department. Customer Retention is the baby of you guessed it, the Customer retention department and marketing is done by the marketing people. This split of responsibility is a legacy of functional specialisation created by relating to business as a production line. Adam Smith wrote in 'The Wealth of Nations' (1776) of an English pin factory.

He described the production of a pin in the following way[xxix]: *"One man draws out the wire, another straightens it, and a third ...will sometime perform two or three of them"*.

The result of labour division in Smith's example resulted in productivity increasing by 240 fold. i.e. that the same number of workers made 240 times as many pins as they had been producing before the introduction of labour division. The insights from Smith underpinned the industrial revolution however using this principle to organise ourselves in the 21st century is to a very large part the wrong approach. That is precisely what the answer to the question will tell us – "sorry sir you are talking to the wrong department, let me transfer you". Or even getting stuck in automated response system hell "press 1 for this, 2 for that, 3 for the other and 4 if you have missed the first three options." These are features of the labour division mind-set. Ask a customer what process they think they are in and you will frequently be surprised by the answer.

Layer 4: What do we do that Impacts customer success?

Often we ask customers to do numerous activities which appear sensible to receive service or indeed buy products. Relating back to the insurance claim we can see rules and procedure around how to make claims, the correct way to complete forms, the process of collating the information, the timeframes within which to claim, the way we can reimburse you and more. Often these restrictions that we imposed made sense at some time in the past however they may no longer be relevant.

The situation is compounded by the way internal functional specialism focus on project objectives. Richard Pebble, a respected New Zealand politician writes in his 1996 book "I've been thinking"[xxx] of the inability of organisations to think clearly of the amount of work they create

> "they spend a million to save a thousand every time"
>
> Richard Pebble

and in fact "they spend a million to save a thousand every time". His story of the challenge within large organisations is typical. The Post Office told me they were having terrible problems tracking telephone lines ... They found an excellent programme in Sweden which the Swedes were prepared to sell them for $2m .... So the managers decided to budget $1m for translating into English and another $1m for contingencies. But, as the general manager explained, it had turned out to be more expensive than the contingency budget allowed and they needed another $7m. "How much", I asked, "have you spent on it so far?" "Thirty-seven million dollars" was the reply. "Why don't we cancel the programme?" I asked "How can we cancel a programme that has cost $37m?" they asked "Do you believe the programme will ever work?" I asked "No, not properly" "Then write me a letter recommending its cancellation and I will sign it" The relief was visible. I signed the letter, but I knew I needed new managers."

This type of inside-out thinking causes companies to create apparently sensible checks and controls within processes that actually manifest as customer inconvenience, cost and delay.

Layer 5: The Successful Customer Outcome – what does the customer really need from us?

At this point we should have enough information to objectively create several statements that articulate the SCO. These statements should be specific, measureable, attainable, relevant and time-bound (SMART). Usually there will 6-10 such statements which become the actual key performance measures as the process moves Outside-In. For example a North American business school completed the SCO

> SCO Statements should be SMART
>
> Specific
> Measurable
> Attainable
> Relevant
> Time-bound

map and created these statements from the customer perspective for an 'Education loan application' process:

a. I need to receive my financial assistance

b. I need to receive aid before the semester starts

c. I need to attend the classes I have chosen

d. I do not want to call to chase progress

e. I need to receive the correct amount

f. I do not want to have to fix your mistakes

There is no ambiguity here and we avoid a common mistake of using management weasel words such as 'efficient, effective, timely' which may mean things internally but to a customer are of little help. Creating SCO statements that may be used as measures for process success is a key aid on the journey to Outside-In.

Layer Six: And now we reach the core of the onion. What is the one line statement that best articulates our Successful Customer Outcome?

This one-liner embodies the very nature of the process and sometimes the business we are in. In 'Thrive - how to succeed in the Age of the Customer'[xxxi] McGregor/Towers (2005), Easyjet (Europe's second largest airline) is used as an example in this quest. Their simple "Bums on Seats" SCO sentence works both from a company perspective (we must maximise utilisation, offer inexpensive seats, and get people comfortably and safely to their destinations) and the customer's needs "I need a cheap safe seat to get me to the sunshine quickly without a fuss".

The company one liner will become part of a series which are measureable through the SCO statements and can be tested and revised depending on evolving customer expectations and needs. It may in fact ultimately replace the inside-out strategic process and provide the organisation with its Raison d'être.

Of course when we start the journey it is often sufficient to create SCO maps to help grow understanding and even if the actual SCO Map is subsequently replaced (as we take a broader view) the improvement in understanding around the customer is invaluable.

3: Reframing process for an Outside-In world

A fundamental principle of Outside-In is the understanding of where your process starts and ends.

In the 20th century many techniques and approaches developed to better understand and create processes.

In its earliest form pioneering work undertaken by the United States Airforce created modelling approaches based on the Structured Analysis and Design Technique (SADT) that produced iDEF (Integrate DEFinition Methods). iDEF became recognised as a global standard as a method designed to model the decisions, actions, and activities of an organisation or system[xxxii].

> The convergence of business process modelling and business process management (BPM) has now produced a rich set of tools and techniques able to model and ideally manage an organisation.

iDEF as a method has now reached iDEF14 [xxxiii] and embraces a wide range of process based modelling ideas. Concurrent with the development of iDEF, technology providers created proprietary modelling approaches, and subsequently developed these into modelling language standards, used by many organisations to represent their systems and ways of working. The convergence of business process modelling and business process management (BPM) has now produced a rich set of tools and techniques able to model and ideally manage an organisation. In fact one of the more accepted definitions of BPM (based on the British Journal of Management[xxxiv]): "Business process management (BPM) is a management approach focused on aligning all aspects of an organisation with the wants and needs of clients. It is a holistic management approach"

Until a few years ago process management practice looked within the boundaries of the organisation and the combination of modelling and management approaches were adequate to understand the enterprise. The impact of process management in improving organisation performance has been profound however we now face a different reality driven by the enlightened customer.

As a consequence both Business Process Management and business process modelling present a series of problems that include

(a) understanding the beginning and end of the process,
(b) the techniques used to model process are inadequate and focused on the wrong things

Strangely customer involvement in a process often appears as an afterthought and the actual representation systems (left to right, top to bottom) create an illusion that fosters the belief that "the customer isn't my job".

Let's deal with each in turn by example:

a. The beginning and end of process

To aid the discussion let's look at two airlines, British Airways and Southwest, and we'll review how they 'think' about their business through the eyes of process. If you sit down with British Airways executives and asked the question "where does your process start

and end?" the response reflects the main source of revenue, ticket sales.

Where does your process start and end?

So the answer "the process is from the ticket purchase to the collecting the bags off the carousel" is no great surprise. In fact that is the way we have mostly thought about process in that

> The Customer Experience is the process.

it starts when it crosses into organisation, and finishes when it leaves. We can easily model that, identify efficiency improvements, improve throughput and optimise apparent value add. This may not be adequate anymore.

As far as British Airways is concerned what you do outside of this process is no concern of theirs, after all they are an airline and that's what they do. Now let's change our perspective and visit Love Field in Texas and meet the executive team of Southwest. Ask the guys the same question "where does your process start and end?" and the answer is a whole different viewpoint.

The process begins when the potential customer thinks of the need for a flight, and only ends when they are back at home following the journey. The scope of this process is defined by the phrase "the customer experience is the process". That's an Outside-In perspective and creates opportunities across the whole customer experience.

More than that it raises the prospect of additional revenue streams, spreads the risk associated with a dependency on ticket sales, reinforces the customer relationship and develops an entirely different way of doing business. So let's ask another question of our friends at Southwest "guys, what business are you in?", and the answer changes everything you ever thought about airlines forever "we're in the business of moving people".

Downstream Southwest may well turn the industry further on its head as they move from being the low cost airline to the 'no cost airline' and give their seats free of charge.

What would that do to your business model if 95% of your revenues, as with British Airways, comes from ticket sales?

The business challenge for Southwest becomes one of controlling the process to benefit and maximise the customer experience. That involves partnering, sharing information and doing all necessary to make customers lives easier, simpler and more successful. Now how do you

model that?

b. The techniques used to model process are inadequate and focused on the wrong things

As we have discussed the ultimate Cause of Work for our organisations is the customer. Organisations exist to serve the customer though the provision of products and services and in this way develops revenue that goes to the profit and onward distribution to the stockholders.

In other organisations without the profit motivation, for instance the public sector, then the effective delivery of services is measured by citizens and stakeholders. Accordingly it stands to reason that everything happening within the organisation should be organised and aligned to deliver customer success. Anything that doesn't contribute is potentially 'dumb stuff'. The techniques we traditionally deploy to 'capture' process are unfortunately not suitable to understanding the causes of work and focus attention instead on visible tasks and activities. In the context of the enlightened customer[xxxv] this is at best misleading and at its worst actually part of the broader problem. In Outside-In companies the focus has shifted to understanding the causes of work, and then engineering those causes to minimize negative effects.

Once more to go Outside-In we need a perspective shift and we can achieve this by identifying those three causes of work and then set out to reveal them and their negative impact.

How big is the size of the prize? Efficiency and productivity gains of 30-60% are common. Cost reduction and margin improvement in the order of 50% is not unusual[xxxvi].

Cause elimination is a seek and destroy mission. It's the challenge to weed out the "dumb stuff" in our organisations.

By truly fixing the Causes of Work, rather than messing around with the Effects we will all make our customers and employees life simpler, easier and more successful.

Are you ready to challenge your assumptions and start eliminating those causes of work? Fix the Cause, remove the effect.

4: Rethinking the business you are in

In the Southwest airlines example we referred to the different viewpoints of the 'business' you are in. The two views – one the organisations, regarded as inside-out, reflect the activities and functions undertaken.

The second viewpoint looks at the business Outside-In, that is from the customers perspective. So British Airways (inside-out) see themselves in the business of flying airplanes and approach the customer with that product/service in mind. They set about marketing and selling the flights and hope to pull the customers to the product through pricing, availability and placement. In a slowly changing world where customers have little choice this strategy can provide a route to success.

As we have already seen the tables have turned and the enlightened customer demands so much more.

Southwest and other Outside-In companies understand this challenge and take the customer viewpoint.

What business would you say these six companies are in: Hallmark Cards, Disney, Zara, AOL, OTIS elevators, China Mobile? Try it from the customers perspective and you'll arrive at a very different answer – try these, expression, joy, style and comfort, community, moving people, connectivity. Yes they are very different and will reframe the way you think of the service and products you provide. Go further and look inside your existing company.

Are you still separated into functional specialist areas providing specific outputs to other departments in the so called 'value chain'? Do you have internal 'service level agreements' that specify what you'll deliver and when? How much of our internal interaction adds ultimate value for the customer? This way of organising work imposes limitations on our ability to truly deliver successful customer outcomes. The Inside-out viewpoint is inefficient, prone to red tape, is extremely risk adverse (checkers checking checkers) and slow in delivering product and service.

Many inside-out organisations regard customers as an inconvenience rather than the reason why they exist.

What business are you in? Past, present, future?

Successful Customer Outcomes - Three Steps to Heaven? Take the Lift

Just the other day I was standing in the lobby of a hotel waiting for the elevator to arrive. I had plenty of thinking time while I waited, and I was reminded of a great recent example of customer-focused innovation. I don't know whether your experience is the same as mine, but I find myself spending a lot of time waiting for elevators to arrive.

This is a common problem in tall buildings with a large number of people – busy elevators have to stop at all floors, slowing their progress and increasing the frustration of those waiting for one to arrive. The answer has often been to put in more elevators, but this causes problems elsewhere notably in the reduction of valuable office space. Some manufacturers and developers have looked to smaller, quicker elevators to alleviate the problem but have come up against capacity issues.

OTIS Elevators took a different view and looked at the way the Japanese railway system works. In Japan, as in many countries, there are both local and express rail services. The difference is that they run on separate tracks meaning that the slow trains do not hold up the express services. When you arrive at the station the train you need is determined by your destination, the time you want to take, and how much you want to pay.

OTIS took that idea and came up with a control panel in the lift lobby – you put in your security card (the mechanism doubles as an ID system), key in the floor that you want to go to and it tells you which lift will get you there the quickest. They have been able to reduce the number of lifts, increase capacity, improve the experience and they now lead the elevator market.

What OTIS Elevators have done is a great example of innovation based on Successful Customer Outcomes (SCOs). To achieve this leap forward in the market they have done three things:

- Understood who their real customers are;
- Worked out what was needed to satisfy these customers;
- Made sure that they can deliver effectively against these SCOs.

It is this combination of getting the SCOs right and making sure that they can be delivered.

We earlier looked at how critical it is to have the customer as the focus of the whole organisations activities. The emphasis isn't just in the words that the organisation uses but in literally everything the company does, from the way that it structures itself, through performance rewards to innovation. Being a business driven by SCOs also means moving away from the constraints of industrial age thinking – big hierarchies, functional stovepipes and limiting improvement to the best practice seen in competitors. Now I will look at three steps that all organisations can take to make the transition to what I call Outside-In.

1. Work out the customers whose needs you are trying to meet, and understand those needs well

A fundamental requirement for defining good SCOs is to make sure you are concentrating on the right "C". You will have heard the phrase "the customer is always right". Well that's not true, at least not in the way that is often used: "every customer is always right"! Some companies are so knotted up with pleasing everybody that they are unable to fully service the needs of the customers that are most important to them.

> Some companies are so knotted up with pleasing everybody that they are unable to fully service the needs of the customers that are most important to them

There are always customers who don't fit well with what a company is trying to do, so be prepared to lose them, so that you can better focus on the customers that you do want. If that sounds like heresy then think in terms of custom rather than customer – there are certain needs that you can't or don't want to meet. It's not the individual that you are dismissing.

It's also important to differentiate between core customers and enabling customers. OTIS Elevators have been successful by focusing on the true customer (the lift user) but without losing sight of the people that buy the equipment they build, the developers and employers. The spark of differentiation comes from delivering to the real end-user; the rest is about getting the delivery right.

So, knowing your customers' needs is a vital part of the process of delivering distinctive offerings. Too many organisations suffer from what I call Customer Attention Deficit Disorder – the inability to focus consistently on customers and their needs. Getting this right needs more than an occasional visit to the frontline or the shop floor. This requires a deep-seated understanding of what is needed throughout the business, not just the results of last week's telephone survey.

> "Everything should be as simple as possible, but no simpler."
> Albert Einstein.

Once you are clear on the customers that you want to serve and what their needs are, the next step involves converting that knowledge into clear objectives.

2. Keep everything clear and simple and focussed on the customer

Consider these two quotations:

- Everything should be made as simple as possible, but not simpler.
- Simplicity is the ultimate sophistication.

These are not the words of slackers. They come from two of the greatest brains in human history, Einstein and Leonardo da Vinci respectively. These two guys could deal with whatever level of complexity confronted them, so this desire for the right level of simplicity had nothing to do with their intellectual ability. If only that were true of many organisations. How often do we see complexity within organisations, in structure, product range or literature, that is worn almost as a badge of distinction?

> Changing a structure without understanding customer needs and how they are to be delivered simply produces a new way of getting things wrong.

Every company needs a clear, concise statement of what it exists to do in terms of Successful Customer Outcomes. SCOs are about bringing the total reality in line with the vision so they must be simple. The more involved they are the more difficult they are to understand and deliver.

As a way of differentiating between good and not so good SCOs, let's look at a recent innovation in car hire. Hertz have developed Neverlost, an in-car GPS navigation service that, as the ad goes, does what it says on the tin. AVIS have introduced an interesting version of this: a mobile 'phone in the car that can be used to contact a call centre for directions! I know which feels like the better solution.

3. Align the organisation to the SCOs

Processes are the delivery mechanisms for SCOs, so getting the processes right is a vital part of the alignment activity. Many companies are looking at their processes and developing process dictionaries and the like, but if this isn't done within the context of SCOs then there is the great risk of just doing the wrong thing more efficiently. There are many techniques available to review and refine processes. What should emerge though isn't a set of projects but an on-going mechanism for ensuring that the company "machinery" is delivering the SCOs.

> functional divisions are a barrier to effective cross-business working

Although it may seem obvious to put the reorganisation element last it is surprising how often this doesn't happen. Changing a structure without understanding customer needs and how they are to be delivered simply produces a new way of getting things wrong. Earlier we looked at how functional divisions are a barrier to effective cross-business working. These stovepipes have been accompanied by a proliferation of specialist teams (look at the emergence of organisation design teams in HR). The inertia created should not be underestimated. Layers of hierarchy also serve to place leaders a long way from where the customer interaction is. Companies built around SCOs don't look like this. They can be, and are, flatter.

The challenge is clear, and we have touched on some of the questions that need answering by organisations that are intent on transforming themselves. There is one particular question that I hear more than any other, although it's not often asked directly: how long has my organisation got to change? Of course there are many answers to this question, answers dictated by market, competition and many other factors.

> How long has my organisation got to change?

I will give my answer to this question by briefly highlighting a great example of wholesale transformation to SCOs. British Telecom (BT) are moving from a cumbersome, inwardly focused hierarchical model to a much more agile output-based structure in less than three years. They are now a market leader in this level of service orientation. If the largest organisations have already turned themselves Outside-In then the companies yet to start will need more than an express lift if they are going to survive .

Despite the upturn many companies won't survive the next two years. That's how long you've got to make sure you are one of the successful Outside-In companies.

Triple Crown plus

Let's talk about simultaneously achieving Increased Revenue, Decreased Cost and Enhanced Customer Service.

While we often "zero in" on one of these BIG THREE metrics of business success, driving forward on all three at the same time is a bridge too far for most.

But what if you knew that these three metrics are intimately linked, that taking action on one will have a direct effect on the other two? Would it surprise you to know that acting to improve one measure commonly causes the other metrics to react in the opposite direction?

Yet eliminating Causes of Work creates simultaneous improvement on all three of these metrics.

Obviously eliminating causes of non-value add work will decrease cost. It will also improve the customer experience by reducing the time of and eliminating points of failure in, customer interactions.

This improved customer experience sends more customers to us by word of mouth.

The result is simultaneous improvement in Revenue, Cost Reduction, and Customer Satisfaction. Focusing on Successful Customer Outcomes pushes the impact even further, delivering the Triple Crown plus. It's the fundamental change at the heart of the most successful companies in the world.

What Price Complexity?

Complexity is insidiously expensive. When production and service cycles take forever, and costs are high, chances are that most of your processes are mired in complexity. Since Victorian times, companies have felt

> Complexity is insidiously expensive

compelled to offer consumers whatever they want, creating a myriad of choice with goods and services each having their own process and production lines. In turn these processes are supported by complex systems and require specific skills for bespoke services and products. How often do you hear the recital "oh we're very different around here. What we are doing is unique in the industry." My response to that? "Oh yes you are unique – just like everyone else." This peculiar

> The biggest enemy of thinking is complexity, for that leads to confusion.
>
> Edward de Bono

'unique view' is to the detriment of the very people you are trying to please - the customer.

Consider a few of the not so hidden costs of complexity:

1. Customer inconvenience – Your customers have to negotiate your complex system and its mind-numbing array of alternatives.
Q. Just how many Moments of Truth are there?

2. Unwieldy sales processes – The sales systems needed to support

complex product lines soon grow too cumbersome, whether they require filling out complicated order forms, getting indecipherable invoices or navigating endless voice mail paths.

Q. How many rules exist to 'guide and direct' and are out of date slowing things to crawl?

Q. How many handoffs occur in your processes between people, systems and services?

Eradicating those Moments of Truth, Business Rules and Breakpoints can change everything.

3. Impact on management – Eventually, even your managers will find numerous products and processes too much to track.

Q. How much money have you spent training people to deal with this complexity?

Remove this complexity and legacy approaches geared to streamlining processes may not be required!

4. As an absolute, the greater an organisation's complexity, the less focused its management.

Q. Where does all that management time get directed? Fire fighting and fixing problems caused by the nightmare of complexity.

Refocus management time to helping align processes for successful outcomes.

You do not have to live with complexity. We have a phrase "Fix the Cause, Remove the Effect" – perhaps that can be your guide also?

Lord Nelson and Successful Customer Outcomes (SCO)

Horatio Nelson is one of the greatest heroes in British history, an honour he earned by defeating Napoleon's fleet in the 1805 Battle of Trafalgar.

The British victory at sea over the French fleet ultimately proved to be the start of the end of the Napoleon era, which finished with another famous battle at Waterloo in 1815.

So what has Lord Nelson got to do with SCO's? To answer that question we need to understand how an out-gunned, out manned and apparently demoralized British fleet could turn the tide of war.

Battles at sea had until Nelsons leadership been conducted by Admirals and Commanders often ashore dispensing orders as if playing a game of chess. Move from here to there and engage that ship. The signals from the command were conveyed by flag wavers, strategically placed across the battle front to provide a visual instruction to ships captains.

Sea battles tended to be well planned and predictable affairs naturally with the fleet with greater resources usually victorious. And so it seemed would be the case as the two largest sea going battle fleets in the world approached a pivotal conflict.

Nelson who was more than familiar with hardship both physical from earlier war wounds (blind in one eye with a crippled arm) and the burdensome politics of the Admiralty brought his captains together to review the battle plans…. Clearly understanding the dilemma he articulated an approach "sink the French fleet at all costs" which in retrospect seems a statement of the blindingly obvious, however tactics and strategy was the domain of the Admirals, not the captains who simply acted out orders provided by flag wavers.

Asking the captains what would that involve brought forward the idea of individual ships acting 'in the moment' to take advantage of the slower moving, albeit more powerful French ships. If the British ships could 'get alongside', rather than waiting for extended orders there was a chance for victory.

And so it was that the flag wavers remained ashore and the captains, seeking to align everything they did to achieve the successful outcome "sink the French fleet" acted in unison and yet with discretion to strike boldly. The rules of the game were changed forever when the British fleet attacked the French in the dead of night. The incredulous French were taken unawares as sea battles traditionally stopped for the night because no one could see the flags….

We can encapsulate Nelsons commitment as just before the battle of Trafalgar he sent a famous signal to his fleet: "England expects every man will do his duty *and sink the French fleet*". Nelson's own last words were "Thank God I have done my duty".

So there we have it. A clear articulation of the successful outcome. An understanding and actioned desire to make that happen through the technology, people and processes. It literally changes the rules of the game – forever.

So how much flag waving goes on in your organisation?

Have you truly articulated the SCO and is everyone and everything aligned to achieving it?

Creating the SCO mind-set

Think of the greatest human achievements, those things that we all acknowledge as new and earth shattering. There were people at the centre making stuff happen, reforming rather than conforming, pushing against the tide of opinion and resisting the momentum of current belief. What did all these people have in common?

> The importance of creating viable options and choices is undeniable: "Let's go this way" has more going for it than "Don't go that way"!

They were masters of mind-set. They knew how to link the old with the new and take people with them into a new way of doing things. Of course the technologies helped, however they were largely developed as a consequence of insight – not as a means to it. They needed people to understand, become committed and then make the vision reality. Those great folks helped to articulate a roadmap that we could trust and follow. At first it just existed in our minds and we then created a new reality.

They all had three qualities in common:

1. Belief that the accepted ways of doing things were no longer appropriate.
2. Conviction that a new way exists that better fits a new order.
3. Courage and tenacity in driving towards that endeavour.

We humans are not natural embracers of change. With some honourable exceptions we tend to favour the continuation of the norm. We may be happy to introduce change to ourselves, but we don't react well when others do it to us.

Uncertainty is often the reason for this resistance, so any change catalyst has to be prepared for rejection and antipathy over a period of time. Uncertainty is temporary though if you work hard enough. Stick with the message and the obstacles will get smaller.

> To be constructive, a critical view needs to incorporate an alternative

Political and shareholder pressure has resulted in extreme short termism. It is estimated that this leads to the average tenure of the CEO in the 21st century being less than three years and accordingly results need demonstrating in double quick time. Senior executives faced with this pressure will often revert to what they know best. It is a popular axiom that the generals in the face of battle will fight the last war again, despite improvements in technology and capability.

History is littered with examples of such failures and yet it seems that in business some CEO's are just as gullible. Witness the recent statements from one CEO of a top three American airline commenting that their industry was really not profitable anymore and at best they are striving for a social service for the most part!

Contrast that with Southwest Airlines performance of 59 quarters out of 61 profit.

If history tells us anything it is that mastering mind-sets can be enormously powerful in effecting major shifts in thought and deed. We can also be sure that some pretty important things wouldn't have happened if everyone had sat around waiting for someone else to start.

What are you doing within your organisation to improve the SCO mind-set?

Disneys take on Outside-In.

Simply Magic.

The average party size to arrive at Disney is five, two adults and

three kids. Disney discovered that many people lock their keys in the car so right at the start they have on-hand a team of professional locksmiths. They drive through the lot looking for distressed families and unlock their cars – free of charge. Simply Magic. Then there's the walk to the gates – but wait. Driving through the crowds are golf carts and helpers to steer you towards the nearest 'magic bus' with colour coded location tags!

You probably get the picture and that's one of the things that makes the Disney performance truly outstanding. The belief that if everything gets itself aligned to the SCO we **reduce cost** (how much effort do you currently apply to fixing stuff that goes wrong that results in queries and non-value added activity?), **drive up revenue** (how many people would you tell?) and **improves customer satisfaction** (would you be pleased?).

Talking about the SCO should be an everyday activity

For many of us talking and acting the SCO way has become second nature. That means if you are eating and breathing the alignment of your processes towards SCO's then progressively the original focus begins to shift and in fact we refine and sharpen our ability both to meet and subsequently exceed customer expectations. That's precisely what is happening in the magic kingdom as we speak. It isn't 'hocus pocus'. It is very direct and is helping Disney achieve that Triple Crown of reducing costs, improving revenues and enhancing service simultaneously. Well I suppose that may seem like weird magic to some. To others it has become a way of life... so how are Disney weaving their spells and moments of magic that draw us and our kids back time after time? At this point let's introduce **Successful Guest Outcomes......**

Successful Guest Outcomes. How does that work then?

For a moment let's reflect on a recent Disney financial report: For the seventh or eighth quarter in a row Walt Disney Co. posted solid revenue, profits and earnings, the performance announced on August 1 in Disney's third quarter financial report,. "I'm pleased to report we had another solid quarter," Disney Chief Executive Officer Robert A. Iger said. "We've again achieved strong results by focusing on doing what we do best: by building high-quality creative franchises across multiple platforms and multiple markets."

Revenue for the quarter of $9.05 billion was up 7 percent compared with the same three months last year. Disney's parks and resorts saw revenue rise 6 percent to $2.9 billion during the quarter, while the segment's operating profit rose 13 percent to $621 million. Those numbers were driven by higher attendance and increased spending by guests, while at the same time maintaining or even lowering some costs of operation, the company reported.

So revenues growing, footfall increasing, costs steady and apparently customer satisfaction on the up. Iger said the parks have succeeded in buffering themselves by offering 'Magic Your Way' tickets and more discount packages to please customers across the whole customer experience process lifecycle.

So it is working then – let's ask ourselves the question how. For this I am going to hand over to a first-hand account from a Neuro Linguistic Programming (NLP) colleague who works and is an expert in the field of brain sciences. His recent personal experience shines a light into the shadows and reveals a simple formula (well most magic potions are just that!) and gives us all cause to reflect on who our customers *really* are.

Tom Hoobyar, NLP Comprehensive, Colorado (reproduced with permission)

The REAL Magic in Disney's Magic Kingdom

Vikki and I were on vacation in Orlando this week, visiting the Disney Magic Kingdom. It was an interesting experience in Attention to Detail. I don't think it was so much the Cinderella makeup kits for little girls and the Mickey Mouse shot glasses in the souvenir shop, or the music everywhere, or even the incredible service at every hotel, restaurant, and even on the shuttle busses that make up the "Magic" part of the Disney Experience.

It was something I've talked about before, but until now I hadn't seen it create a billion dollar impression. It was the language they use. No, it's English all right, but they have special words for things that are different from the words the rest of the world uses. I don't know if you're aware of it, but I noticed it when we arrived at Epcot Centre - one of the Disney parks located in the centre of Florida. I saw a man push a utility cleaning cart through a door marked "Cast Members only". Hmmmm. "Cast members?" The guy was a janitor...

Read Tom's full review at www.tomhoobyar.com/news/

To coin a phrase the Successful Customer Outcome is a gift that just keeps on giving.

How do you ease the way for your customers and make it a pleasurable experience?

Reach a New Service Altitude

I've been flying regularly for 25 years or more, and in the last twelve months I've clocked up over 350,000 miles; my lifetime mileage must be reaching interplanetary

levels. I've travelled (and often grappled) with nineteen different airlines in the last 12 months, so I feel pretty well qualified to provide my take on what the airline industry should be doing to make the customer experience significantly better.

I'm going to concentrate here on airline examples of what are known as 'Next Practice'. These are ideas that go beyond simply emulating the best efforts of the competition. The more progressive companies are already testing some new offerings and proving through sustained customer loyalty that it is possible to prosper while traditional incumbents stumble and fail.

And yet with the current malaise affecting some of the old airlines what are they considering doing to reduce cost? They are going to remove their primitive over-hanging screens to save on weight! Wow, that's really going to help win more business and give them a viable future (not).

The World's largest Airlines

1 - American Airlines

2 - United Airlines

3 - Delta Air Lines

4 - Air France

5 - Continental Airlines

6 - Lufthansa

7 - Southwest Airlines

8 - British Airways

9 - Northwest Airlines

10 - Emirates

Source: International Air Transport Association. Calculated on total passenger miles flown

easyJet and the sick bag

This may not sound like a promising place to start, but bear with me. easyJet, a European budget airline, continues to grow at the expense of many of its rivals.

These include the large international monoliths who have until recently operated with some impunity with regard to passenger comfort and fares. In an environment of rising fuel costs, terrorist threat, increasing competition and inflexible organisation structures, bottom line cost performance has become critical. This is even more pertinent for the budget carriers, where seemingly inexpensive items represent a large proportion of the ticket price. Many airlines have haphazardly reduced the offer to reduce the cost; easyJet have looked to innovate.

Taking an idea from Southwest Airlines, who advertise job vacancies on their sick bags, easyJet have gone that step further into Next Practice and removed the cost of the sick bags by getting someone else to pay for them. Kodak provide the bags, which if unused can be employed as film envelopes for those vacation pictures. Even in this digital age many folk are wedded to their 35mm cameras. For the digitally liberated, Kodak also provide fast turnaround development services for photo media – you guessed it, right there in the arrivals lounge. Easyjet of course can focus clearly on this type of opportunity because their Successful Customer Outcome, as articulated by their creator, Stelios, is "Bums on Seats".

So what SCO-inspired survival tips can we propose that may help the troubled airline giants to survive, if it isn't already too late?

Easy Upgrades

For some airlines this is a contradiction in terms. I travelled on a major national airline recently and discovered the phenomenon of the non-upgradeable ticket. Bounced between check-in and the "Customer Service Desk" (another contradiction in terms) I learned that I "had bought the wrong ticket" and "didn't understand how these things worked". Faced with the choice of paying again for a completely new ticket or accepting my fate, I chose the latter and spent the flight grumpily eyeing the empty Business Class seats from the crowded Economy cabin. Needless to say I won't be warming the seats of that particular airline again.

Contrast this with an experience on another airline where my request to upgrade using frequent flyer miles was met with "that's OK sir, I'll upgrade you without taking the miles". The difference is not better process or rules – it's a question of culture.

And this highlights one of the key points that emerged as I sifted through my travel experiences for this article. Some of the most striking experiences I have had have come from individuals being able to do the right thing (even the unexpected thing) when it matters. A flight attendant who apologises for the fact that we are not flying on one of the brand new aircraft in the fleet (but which is still better than most); the generous and immediate compensation for a mid-flight entertainment system failure. These responses come from liberated staff in customer-focused organisations.

Successful Customer Outcomes come from, and are delivered through people. Those folks should be given the opportunity to innovate to be great.

Can we recommend any Airlines?

For fellow travellers I have noted my experience over the last year or two and naturally my choices are driven by people who meet and exceed my expectations.

Consistently good on the routes I fly are:

Emirates, Virgin Atlantic, Virgin America, Kingfisher, Singapore Airlines, and Continental (so much improved recently). And it would be churlish not to mention the dogs of the industry. Any of these airlines may choose to move 'Outside-In' with immediate effect rather than regard the customer as somewhat of an inconvenience.

British Airways, Iberia, KLM/Air France, Aer Lingus, America Airways, Air India, Qantas, United and Qatar (their on-board TV advert that talks of 5 star service. Great if you are one of the four people 'up front' but for the other 300 passengers very irritating).

What would your list of innovations look like? Have you ever been asked? I wonder.

Public Sector Outside-In?

Government departments at all levels need to be very clear on who the customer is and what they want. In this they are no different from a private enterprise. Customers do not care about your internal bureaucracy or your policies and  procedures, they do care about being able to access your services in an efficient manner and know that they are being cared for.

Nobody is suggesting for one moment that you can please everybody. But if those that you are not pleasing are displeased through poor service or overly complicated procedures and policies then they have in most cases good cause to complain. Indeed, employees in the public sector would do well to remember that it is their tax money that is being potentially wasted too!

Many people might feel that government and public sector is "different" and that the same rules cannot apply. To a small extent this may be right, but in the majority of cases fresh thinking can still lead to significantly increased service, lower costs and improved efficiency.

For example take the case of the Chicago Works Department and how they transformed a moribund public service (fixing potholes) which typically took 6-8 weeks, involved up to 30 people, and on average cost an incredible $42,000 USD is now legend in BPM parlance[xxxvii].

Daniel Pink (A Whole New Mind[xxxviii]) would be proud of the right brain thinking which imported Expedia's scheduling 'idea' to let citizens define the problem, chose a suitable repair and select a convenient date for the repair team fix from a two screen web based system. Problem fixed. Now on average 4 days, 5 people and $2,000 USD. That still seems a lot (especially for tax payers) for filling a hole but boy is it giant step in the right direction!

The full story of the fix will wait for another day however the quantum leap here with next practice and Successful Customer Outcomes drew its inspiration from Expedia.

Of course we can extend this thinking even further into many walks of public service.

Where would you start your next practice endeavours?

A very old question, a very new Answer

At a recent senior executive seminar a Chief Operating Officer in a large retail company asked

"How can we make sure our people follow through and continually deliver the right thing? So often our initiatives start well and then people take their eye off the ball." There were nods of agreement all round.

And then came a spirited response from a progressive Airline Executive (think geography and go where the birds go in a Northern US Winter) and his suggestion was so simple it was surprising that so few get it. "Well we reward for success. That is the achievement of the SCO and everyone in our company is linked to that goal. And I mean everyone right on down from the CEO to the newest trainee and college recruit."

> Is everything you are doing aligned with achieving the SCO? If it isn't then challenge those non-aligned tasks and activities and stop doing the dumb stuff

It set the room into a frenzy of debate, some folks insisting they do that already, others asking for more detail and some saying tried that and still failed. Airline Executive continued sensing he had something of major interest to contribute, "you see everything you do through the experience and expectation of the customer. I know we have talked about that for years but how often do we follow through, even on things like 'Voice of the Customer' in Lean and Six Sigma we paid lip service to the effort to truly understand and articulate everything through the SCO." He had everyone's attention now and continued, "Once you get started and have a clear explanation of your SCO ask yourself the question 'is everything we are doing aligned with achieving this SCO?" – if it isn't challenge it and ultimately stop doing the dumb stuff."

We then had a thirty minute brainstorm of relevant SCOs to realize that at the start there are more than a few, lots in fact. Some apparent SCOs are simply not so. Take the one suggested by a well-meaning banker "To deliver credit cards on time within budget." Initially that creates an illusion of working towards mutual success but on closer examination this one is 'inside out' and really doesn't care too much about the customer. The real SCO revolves around creating the capability for a customer to use their facility in a simple trouble freeway. When you think of it 'Outside-In' that takes you to a whole new place with a set of new answers to some very old questions.

The discussion was in danger of running over time so we all took away a brief to 'search and deploy' our respective SCOs knowing that our first efforts would be iterative and a learning experience.

Our next meeting then focused on helping people align to the SCO and doing as the Airline Executive proposed – rewarding folks for achieving those SCOs.

How would you do that?

Where in Process Management is the Customer?

At a time where customer satisfaction and loyalty have reached historic lows, and competition has reached its historical peak, the question must be asked, "where in Process Management is the customer?"

Yes, the customer is a missing piece in the vast majority of Process Management practices (Six Sigma, Lean and Business Process Management)

Management principles have traditionally approached business success from the inside-out perspective, concentrating on margin-based improvements. That made a lot of sense during the time when internal activities suffered from substantial bloat and competition was limited by geography and time to market.

Yet over the years we have dipped into that well many times, and the well is about to run dry. Some statistics suggest as we continue to try to achieve the same percentage of gain through each improvement cycle, each iteration produces significantly less tangible value to the organisation. It's a funnel affect that just gets narrower and narrower through every cycle, leaving less and less real benefit for the business.

Meanwhile what is really driving business success? The answer, of course, is the customer. In the 21st Century Value Chain it is the number of customers and the lifecycle of the business-customer relationship that determines business success.

Known as Customer Expectation Management (CEM) and Outside-In, the setting of customer expectations and the delivery of those expectations without exception is the "secret sauce" behind the success of market-leading companies such as Virgin, Fedex, Zara, Best Buy, and Southwest Airlines, to name a few.

Outside-In companies are able to progressively and continually innovate and create clear water between themselves and rivals and in many instances becoming market leaders. That's what US based Bust Buy did with their Customer Centricity strategy. That's what FedEx Kinko are doing with their massively simplified 'idea to delivery' process. This is what Virgin Group do across their network of more than one hundred companies.

> There is no place where customers are less loyal and more demanding than in the arena of lowest price decision buying

Many of these market leaders are not competing on price. Sure, their prices are competitive but that is not where their success lies. In many cases they are even able to charge a premium for their products because they are setting and managing customer expectations with a vengeance. They are telling customers what to expect, making their customers' lives simpler and easier while delivering on these expectations with consistency.

Meanwhile, price competitors are stuck in a no-holds barred dogfight for the worst customer any business can have, the customer who buys predominately by price. There is no place where customers are less loyal and more demanding than in the arena of lowest-price decision buying.

Taking Customers to Heart

Yet process management by and large doesn't include the customer except as an adjunct to inside-out activities. Improving quality and streamlining processes can help reduce really  poor customer experiences or align a business with the market expectation a competitor has set. But these are only secondary effects of the goals in reducing internal costs, increasing worker productivity and so on.

In an age verging on unlimited choice, global competition, and enlightened customers often livid with dissatisfaction, the only way to be a market leader is to be a customer leader. We all know that our businesses must have customers and we have all had our share of unsatisfactory customer experiences. In spite of this, why is it so difficult for us to quit viewing our business from the inside-out? Habit and tradition is all that is holding us back. Will we allow our history to determine our future? It's our choice.

Is there a way to know if the customer is really part of the process practice? Absolutely. Take a look at your business processes. All business processes have an outcome, right? So how many of your business processes have a customer outcome? What about the concept of a successful customer outcome (SCO)?

To fulfil its destiny of being the Next-Generation Business Enabler that its proponents want it to be, Process management must realign its focus to the customer. Business processes must focus on the customer, minimize potential points of failure (such as Moments of Truth which yield either moments of magic or moments of misery), and produce successful customer outcomes at all points where the customer touches the business.

That's the essence behind Customer Expectation Management and Outside-In. It is the critical element in the drive to increase growth and profitability. Traditional inside-out process improvement leverages customer success by maximizing the net positive effect to the organisation's bottom line but it won't create success by itself.

The only reason we are here is to serve our customers and by serving our customers, making their lives simpler and easier, and helping them be successful we will make our businesses successful.

It's simple and straightforward. Focusing on the customer from the customer's point of view is our opportunity to achieve the success we all want. It's the experience we all want when we are in the role of the customer. It should be at the heart of everything we do and should be woven into the fabric of every application and system we use.

Will Enterprise process management be a cornerstone in the creation of success for your business? It could be, but the question you should be asking yourself is far simpler:

Is the customer at the heart of your process management plan?

Conclusion

Reality is in the eyes of the beholder.

Everyone sees and perceives things differently to the extent that witnessing an objective event will produce multiple versions of the same things. Some abstract, others detailed, some deep, some broad. All are different and yet they are the same thing. So it is with Outside-In.

We each filter everything through our personal experience and it is this experience, accumulated as history, that determines what we believe an objective event to be.

If your experience is a limiting one then in all likelihood you will see yourself as limited, the universe as limited, and change a difficult and scary thing. If on the other hand your experience tells you that you are boundless you will see the universe as a place for opportunity, growth and limitless with incredible possibilities.

Why should we let history dictate our future? If your experience has been a limited one then here is the opportunity to free yourself from the shackles of the past. Whatever you believed about yourself in the past you are not mandated to continue that way into the future. If you and your company are to survive in this period of turmoil you must indeed change, so embrace the opportunity and see the future for what it is – a place of unlimited possibility.

To be truly Outside-In we need to embrace the total customer experience and correspondingly free ourselves of the shackles of history, red tape, cost, needless complexity and inward focus. Move forward boldly on behalf of the customer and make them the centre of our universe.

Remember the customer is the only reason our organisations exist. If they go away so do you.

If you do so, you too will join the leading companies of the 21st century and your life will become easier, simpler and more successful.

"The greater danger for most of us lies not in setting our aim too high and falling short; but in setting our aim too low, and achieving our mark."

Michelangelo

Overview of some of the companies that are actively moving Outside-In

Apple	Hallmark Cards
Bank Santander	H&M
BestBuy	Nordstrom
BMW	OTIS Elevators
Cabela's	Pickfords
Capital One	PolyOne
Chicago Works Department	Proctor & Gamble
China Mobile	Prudential
Disney	Ryan Air
Easyjet	South West
Emirates	State Farm
FedEx Kinko	Tesco
Four Seasons	Virgin Atlantic
Gilead Science	Virgin Mobile
Google	Zara

About the BP Group

To give you some context my exposure with BPM as a management approach goes back to 1992 when I co-founded the precursor to the 'not for profit' BP Group with a group of senior executives in the US and Europe. As part of that initiative I wrote a book in 1993/4 – 'BPR – A Practical Handbook for Executives'[xxxix], in the course of the associated seminars coined the term – Business Process Management. Before that we had 'process management', 'business processes' and of course 'business management' but not the phrase BPM. Since then I have authored and contributed to several books so naturally I have a passion over our collective understanding!

Firstly BPM is not (just) a technology. It's a management approach that includes strategy, people, processes and technology. As such its scope, to quote Andrew Spanyi, 'stretches from the board room to the lunch room'[xl]. The effective deployment of a BPM strategy transforms business, and in fact organisations like Virgin, South West, Capital One and Best Buy embrace a wide definition and will indeed deploy several technologies to help them achieve their objectives.

It is a fact of life that some people hijack definitions such as BPM and market their narrow interpretation as the real thing. Then as those things fail or underperform people say 'tried that and it didn't work – what's next?'. Hence through the BP Group we undertake research to track progress, and in 2008 published that research[xli] .

Subsequently we have further defined Enterprise/Advanced Process Management as the evolution of BPM. Some of those advanced ideas were discussed in the co-authored book 'Customer Expectation Management' in 2006[xlii] .

As part of the BP Groups' broader endeavour we work closely with senior management and continue to develop and refine our understanding of BPM in its many forms. Through the BP Group this understanding is shared with the community and collectively we can all ensure a focus on practical success and delivery. That will more than anything else underline the value of effective BPM.

This collective quest is an excellent one and will potentially gain greater traction if the 'technology' appears as part of a broader solution. Finally take with a large pinch of salt the commentary of the Analysts, who are after all paid by the IT vendors and tend to publish less than impartial views.

To find out more:

Community - www.bpgroup.org – the home page of the community established in 1992
More than 40,000 members across the globe

LinkedIn – www.linkedin.com/groups?gid=1062077 - Daily discussions and articles

Outside-In resources - www.oibpm.com – people, consultancy and support for those aspiring to Outside-In

Training and Coaching - www.bp2010.com – the place to enrol for training and Certification in Advanced BPM and Outside-In
Join more than 10,000 Certified Process Professionals™ in 118 countries

Resources from this book – www.outsideinthesecret.com – find out more, download templates and the CEMMethod™

About the Author

A seasoned practitioner with over 30 years of hands-on experience, Steve is one of industry's noted experts in Enterprise BPM and Performance transformation. He heads the Research & Professional Services network within the BP Group.

As a co-founder of BP Group in 1992 Steve developed the world's first and premier network for Process & Performance professionals. Now in 118 countries with membership of 30,000+. The BP Group has offices in London, Houston, Bangalore & Sydney.

A noted leader Steve works as a mentor, coach and consultant and has helped pioneer through research and 'hands-on' exposure to the world's leading companies, the evolution to Advanced BPM aka 'Outside-In '. Recently recognised as a global thought leader in 'Outside-In' Steve continues to evolve process thinking towards a customer centric view of business.

An inspirational speaker (he has chaired and keynoted at more than 20 international conferences since 2001), contributor to leading journals and author of several books including:

- A Senior Executives Guide to BPR (1994)
- In Search of BPM Excellence (2004)
- Thrive! How to Succeed in the Age of the Customer" (2005)
- CEM - Success without Exception (2006)
- Outside-In. The secret of the 21st century leading companies (2010)

Steve previously worked for Citibank where he led restructuring and business process transformation programs both in the US and Europe.

As a recognised authority in the arena of business performance improvement Steve sits as a judge on several global Award programme including the annual North America Process Excellence & Lean Six Sigma Award panel, the annual European Process Excellence Award jury and the Chair of the Enterprise Architecture & IT Awards (In conjunction with iCMG & Zachman International). In addition he advises several boards across the globe and sits on the steering panel of the influential California based BPM Forum, a group of distinguished CXO's heading up Global 500 companies.

He received the "Lifetime Achievement Award for contribution to Business" at Gartners Annual Summit in 2007.

Steve lives with his wife Penny and family in the UK and US.

Read of recent work at http://www.stevetowers.com and reach him

at steve.towers @ bpgroup.org

Bibliography

[i] http://en.wikipedia.org/wiki/List_of_mobile_network_operators

[ii] http://www.amazon.com/Information-Payoff-Transformation-Work-Electronic/dp/0029317207

[iii] http://www.amazon.com/Reengineering-Corporation-Manifesto-Business-Revolution/dp/088730687X

[iv] The Age of Customer Capitalism, by Roger Martin – HBR Jan-Feb 2010

[v] http://www.southwest.com/about_swa/press/factsheet.html#funFacts

[vi] C.Britt Beemer, Robert L. Shook in 'The Customer Rules: The 14 Indispensible, Irrefutable, and Indisputable Qualities of the Greatest Service Companies in the World'

[vii] http://www.fedex.com/us/office/

[viii] Wikipedia

[ix] Harvard Business Review, July 1990, pp 104–112

[x] 'What killed BPR? Some evidence from the literature' Eric Deakins, Hugh H. Makgill, Business Process Management Journal, V3 1997.

[xi] Tennant, Geoff (2001). SIX SIGMA: SPC and TQM in Manufacturing and Services. Gower Publishing, Ltd.. p. 6. ISBN 0566083744

[xii] De Feo, Joseph A.; Barnard, William (2005). *JURAN Institute's Six Sigma Breakthrough and Beyond - Quality Performance Breakthrough Methods*. Tata McGraw-Hill Publishing Company Limited.

[xiii] BPGroup Research 2008 via LinkedIn

[xiv] Toyota Production System, Ohno, Taiichi, 1988, Productivity Press

[xv] http://www.polyone.com/en-us/Pages/default.aspx

[xvi] http://www.amazon.com/Customer-Expectation-Management-Success-Exception/dp/092965207X

[xvii] Customer Expectation Management (2006)
http://www.amazon.com/exec/obidos/ASIN/092965207X/httpwwwstevet-20

[xviii] P62. The General Theory of Employment, Interest and Money (1935), John Maynard Keynes, English Economist (1883-1946)

[xix] http://www.amazon.com/Screw-Lets-Do-Lessons-Quick/dp/0753510995/httpwwwstevet-20

[xx] US Department of Transportation - http://www.bts.gov/press_releases/2009/bts059_09/pdf/bts059_09.pdf

[xxi] Richard Branson (1999) Losing My Virginity: How I've Survived, Had Fun, and Made a Fortune Doing Business My Way - http://www.amazon.com/Losing-My-Virginity-Survived-Business/dp/0812932293

[xxii] Peter Fingar - http://www.peterfingar.com/

[xxiii] Process Excellence conference, London 2006

[xxiv] http://sundaytimes.lk/071028/FinancialTimes/ft3017.html

[xxv] http://en.wikipedia.org/wiki/Richard_Normann

[xxvi] http://www.amazon.com/Moments-Truth-Jan-Carlzon/dp/0063120976/

[xxvii] http://www.daniweb.com/news/story218685.html

[xxviii] The Hawthorne effect is an effect whereby subjects improve an aspect of their behaviour being measured simply in response to the fact that they are being studied not in response to any particular experimental manipulation.
The term was coined in 1955 by Henry A. Landsberger when studying experiments during 1924-1932 at the Hawthorne Works factory in Chicago. Hawthorne Works had commissioned a study to see if its workers would become more productive in higher or lower levels of light. The workers' productivity seemed to improve when changes were made and slumped when the study was concluded. It was suggested that the productivity gain was due to the motivational effect of the interest being shown in them. Thus the term is used to identify any type of short-lived increase in productivity.

[xxix] Adam Smith wrote in 'The Wealth of Nations' "One man draws out the wire, another straightens it, a third cuts it, a fourth points it, a fifth grinds it at the top for receiving the head: to make the head requires two or three distinct operations: to put it on is a particular business, to whiten the pins is another ... and the important business of making a pin is, in this manner, divided into about eighteen distinct operations, which in some manufactories are all performed by distinct hands, though in others the same man will sometime perform two or three of them".

[xxx] http://www.amazon.com/Ive-been-thinking-Richard-Prebble/dp/1869581709

[xxxi] http://www.amazon.com/Thrive-How-Succeed-Age-

Customer/dp/092965241X/httpwwwstevet-20

[xxxii] http://www.idef.com/IDEF0.htm

[xxxiii] http://en.wikipedia.org/wiki/IDEF

[xxxiv] Understanding Business Process Management: implications for theory and practice, British

Journal of Management (2008) (Smart, P.A, Maddern, H. & Maull, R. S.)

[xxxv] See chapter The Enlightened Customer

[xxxvi] http://images.businessweek.com/ss/09/03/0326_bw50/51.htm

[xxxvii] www.certifiedprocessprofessional.com

[xxxviii] http://www.amazon.com/Whole-New-Mind-Information-Conceptual/dp/1573223085

[xxxix] http://tinyurl.com/6y2t9s

[xl] http://www.amazon.com/Search-BPM-Excellence-Straight-Thought/dp/0929652401

[xli] http://www.towersassociates.com/Towers_Associates_Process_Excellence_Evolution.html

[xlii] http://www.amazon.com/exec/obidos/ASIN/092965207X/httpwwwstevet-20

Lightning Source UK Ltd.
Milton Keynes UK

172787UK00005B/9/P

9 780956 513502